Struggles In (Elderly) Care

Hanne Marlene Dahl

Struggles In (Elderly) Care

A Feminist View

palgrave
macmillan

Hanne Marlene Dahl
Department of Social Sciences and Business
Roskilde University
Roskilde, Denmark

ISBN 978-1-137-57760-3   ISBN 978-1-137-57761-0   (eBook)
DOI 10.1057/978-1-137-57761-0

Library of Congress Control Number: 2017946323

Cover illustration: ipopba/Getty

Printed on acid-free paper

This Palgrave Macmillan imprint is published by Springer Nature
The registered company is Macmillan Publishers Ltd.
The registered company address is: The Campus, 4 Crinan Street, London, N1 9XW, United Kingdom

Contents

1 Introduction   1

2 The Changing Landscape of Elderly Care and
   the Proliferation of Struggles   27

3 Theorizing Elderly Care   61

4 Silences That Matter   89

5 Regulating Elderly Care And Struggles   115

6 Conclusion: A New Analytics   159

Index   175

1

Introduction

In Roskilde and Rome, and in Beijing, Berlin and Brussels, struggles about elderly care are taking place. The issues around which these struggles are many: Who should we care for? What is 'proper care' and how should it be regulated? Who should provide the care? And what kind of working conditions should caregivers endure? By struggles I refer to clashes at the individual and collective levels—not involving violence or weapons—that may stem from disagreements, tensions between social processes, discourses and between different policy goals and different logics in care practices and resistance to existing discourses by individuals, groups and/or social movements.

Some of the issues mentioned above have turned into collective struggles. In 2007 in Denmark, for example, home helps and municipal staff charged with caring for the elderly protested in front of the Danish parliament, carrying banners saying: 'Union of Disregarded Workers', 'Poor and Overworked' and 'Time to Care' (Dahl 2009). In Finland, there have been struggles over a new elderly care act (Hoppania 2015) following media scandals about deficiencies in elderly care. Between 2010 and 2014 Finnish politicians and other stakeholders debated the framing of a new elderly care law. Originally, the new legislation was justified as a response to insufficient resources and poor quality care. However,

© The Author(s) 2017
H.M. Dahl, *Struggles In (Elderly) Care*,
DOI 10.1057/978-1-137-57761-0_1

during these struggles, the problem of elderly care was reframed as one of insufficient legislation. The original problem was forgotten, and elderly care was de-politicized (Hoppania 2015). The Finnish and Danish examples are not unique. In Sweden and Norway as well, there have been struggles about elderly care spurred by neo-liberalism and the effect of New Public Management (NPM)[1] reforms and the need to ensure the rights of elderly people (Vabø and Szebehely 2012). These examples illustrate the kinds of struggles about elderly care taking place in Nordic countries, but the Nordic cases are not exceptions.

Outside the Nordic welfare states, in countries with varying political constellations, struggles have taken place concerning care of the elderly and the working conditions for caregivers. In Great Britain, struggles over elderly care have centered on the formal recognition of informal care, that is, caregiving by family/close others. Carers UK, an organization of those caring for the sick and elderly, has instigated a campaign about the use of the positively valorized word of 'carer' to be exclusively used by family carers (Lloyd 2006), arguing that the government should grant the kind of labor rights to informal carers to ensure their working conditions, including pension rights. At the EU level, the organization 'Eurocarers' was formed as an interest organization for unpaid family carers (Williams 2010). Struggles over elderly care can also be observed in continental European and Mediterranean countries. In Rome, live-in workers from Eastern Europe struggle for proper working conditions while working in the midst of families and caring for the Italian elderly at the same time. These migrant workers struggle to receive vacation benefits and with their host families about providing adequate care (Isaksen 2011).

Struggles over elderly care are not limited to Europe. In China struggles about elderly care concern the role of children (typically the single child) and his/her responsibilities to either provide or finance the care of elderly parents. The Chinese state frames the issue of elderly care not as a question of state responsibility, but of the child's (children's) responsibility. The state provides normative guidance and governance through its publication and dissemination of an instruction manual of how to care for one's parents. In the manual, the state urges the child (children) to uphold family obligations of care for one's parents and to purchase health insurance (Jacobs and Century 2012): Here the political solution is to promote familialism,[2] marketization (buying health and care insurance) and ensure that these obligations are enforced through law. Chinese law now codifies moral obligations and sanctions any adult child who does not care for his/her parents.

These examples illustrate the kinds of struggles over elderly care that we find in many parts of the world. Nearly everywhere the 'elder burden' and the 'demographic challenges' are at the top of the national, political agenda. This is not a coincidence inasmuch as sociopolitical problems can become transnational discourses, traveling around the globe. Nation states are increasingly part of a more global form of governance, interacting in international organizations such as the World Health Organization (WHO) and the Organisation for Economic Co-operation and Development (OECD) or in intergovernmental organizations such as the EU. Through these forums, there occurs a spill-over effect by which problem framings, solutions and best practices are promoted, and then imported or translated into the specific institutional context of the nation state in question. These international organizations themselves are not devoid of internal conflicts about the issues they seek to solve, nor do the international organizations always understand the problem of elderly care in precisely the same way. Hence, we observe struggles within states, within and between international organizations, and between the elderly in need of care, their family members and the care worker/professional carer.

The Proliferation and Intensification of Struggles

The intensification and proliferation of struggles about elderly care reflect a profound global transformation of elderly care. This transformation tends to create uncertainty and tensions that can fuel resistance and struggles among the various stakeholders in the elder care regime. Hence, we witness dramatically changing conditions of care, heightened expectations about what proper care should be, and increasing discussions about the quality of care. The changing conditions, I will argue, involve seven social and political processes: commodifying, globalizing, professionalizing, de-gendering, bureaucratizing, neo-liberalizing and late modernizing. These processes are not inevitable, but they are mediated and translated by agency. Instead of nouns I use verbs to indicate that they are political processes and not deterministic. The intersection of these seven processes creates more fragmentation, insecurity of care and clashes between different logics.[3] Processes that will be elaborated in Chap. 2 of this book. Logics are not understood as something inherent and stable in social life, as in the immanent, ideal-typical rationalities behind social action in Weber's social theory (Weber 1921) or in the 'rationality of care' as understood in the work of Wærness (1987). Instead, logics are dynamic ways of seeing and arguing that can only be identified empirically. Here I am inspired by the Dutch philosopher Annemarie Mol, who defines a logic as a rationale of the practices that are appropriate to do at a particular site or in a particular situation (Mol 2008: 8). Following Mol, a given field of care and a logic of care do *not* exist in themselves. Rather, there is a field of care[4] with vulnerable bodies traversed by different logics in time and space.

The conditions of possibility for care are dynamic. However, care is also increasingly being discussed in various contexts. This discussion derives from the fact that care has now moved out of, and away from, the domestic or intimate sphere and is now a global policy issue. Care policies, standards and practices are now being discussed in policy forums as diverse as those in Beijing, Brussels, Gothenburg, Geneva, Madrid, Manila, Rome, Roskilde and Washington—to name but a few. As Williams (2010) has noted, care has emerged as a 'political concern'; care is increasingly being discussed in political assemblies (parliaments, governments, municipalities). However, care is also part of what is termed 'the political'; the conflictual element constituted by the boundary between the social and the political. Here I draw on Chantal Mouffe's understanding of the political (2005). Whereas the social consists of the sedimented (frozen) social practices, the political arises at the very moment that one of these social practices is questioned. In this sense, the political is based on an unstable and changing boundary between the social and the political. Questioning existing practices or values makes the political visible—and creates a moment of openness (Hoppania and Vaittinen 2015). It is at this juncture that existing care practices become political or contested.

Care has left the exclusively private sphere and entered the social sphere. Care is now paid, managed, regulated and professionalized (Arendt 1958; Tronto 1993; Stone 2000; Johansson 1994; Dahl 2000a, 2010; Williams 2010). In contrast to an earlier era, care is now spoken about in politics and in the political. Care is no longer silenced; it is increasingly visible—it is brought into existence in the articulation of ideas and political deliberation by the increasing proliferation of discourses about care. Discourses form and limit the understandings available and in so doing, they constitute a horizon of understanding. Such a horizon limits what can be said and done, including the positions that persons can occupy legitimately (Norval 1996: 4). In this way the discourse limits the objects being dealt with, the subject positions that agents can occupy and the legitimate ways of arguing.[5]

By 'struggles' I refer to clashes at the individual and collective levels and they do not necessarily imply an intention by the individual agents—as struggles can arise suddenly, as a reaction to a particular practice. This reaction can take the form of 'resistance' a broad concept that could include inaction, persistence, dissent, counterforce, and interruption or in the most radical case, rebellion (Bröckling et al. 2010: 18–19). For example, some hospital doctors resist filling out forms that are part of a new regime of quality control and standardization. For them, the work of treating patients, some in acute danger, is more important than doing what they view as meaningless paperwork (Rasmussen 2012). The resistance of doctors consists of inaction toward required processes of documentation. In Austria and Italy, care workers are working within families and care for elderly family members through state financed cash-for-care schemes given to the families. Domestic workers—such as those in Austria or Italy—around the globe have struggled to become included in unions and to have their work, much of it intimate personal care, regulated more globally, such as through the International Labor Organization (ILO). These struggles were successful in 2011, with the decision of a 'Domestic Workers Convention'. Social movements, such as the women's movement and the disability movement, have also fought to bring care to the political agenda and to form care according to specific values. The focus of this book will be on paid care. As such, paid care is part of a care market, where professional carers, designated care workers and some family members are paid a wage or a sum of money. Being paid *can* become politicized and thereby public. By becoming public, care can be related to regulation in the broad sense, that is, to the state and state institutions. Struggles about boundaries of the state (to care or not to care?) take place in the debates about division of responsibilities between the state and civil society (read: families and close others) or between the state and the market. Boundaries between the state and the 'outside' are not as solid as they used to be. With market-based services paid by the state (in the form of vouchers), cash-for-care and new forms of cooperation between the state, private firms and Non-Governmental Organizations (NGOs), such as Private Public Partnerships (PPP), it becomes increasingly difficult to determine the state and its boundaries. Provision of care is a regulatory gray area.

Struggles are interesting to study, as they have not been studied in the otherwise extensive research on care. Recently, some researchers have focused on struggles in relation to care (Newman and Tonkens 2011). Research to date has shown the contradiction between different rationalities (Wærness 1987) and the clash between different worlds (Stone 2000). The contradictions and dilemmas have been seen as inevitable. These struggles have been interpreted as being difficult—and impossible—choices between alternatives. Here I want to introduce a different view. I focus analytically on struggles within care and about care (see Chap. 3 for an elaboration). I see contradictions and dilemmas as frozen struggles that need to be seen in a more dynamic way. These frozen struggles, I argue, are in fact clashes between different and changing logics. Struggles point to conflicts and points of change between the 'old' and the 'new' order, as when the state takes on new responsibilities—or reduces them—for elderly people, or when new forms of providing care are generated. Struggles are renegotiations of established positions and identities and in this way also indicative of something new. They are a part of the day-to-day activities in social systems and as such part of its nearly invisible reproduction. On the other hand, struggles are sites of resistance against policy initiatives and new policy instruments or toward conflicts about the introduction of regulation, protection, new values and state responsibility. In such situations, struggles result in incremental or even transformative changes. Sometimes policy initiatives embody different logics, leading to tensions and perhaps even to modifications in order to reduce tensions, or perhaps to struggles between these different ways of viewing and providing care. Struggles are about who we are and will be; they are about power, identities and affective involvement. To focus more on struggles enables us to get a more dynamic picture of care and of the processes of change that lie behind changing logics. Struggles also point to the micro-cosmos of change and where the political is also made (Foucault 1978). Politics is not just made by governments or in international forums. Politics is made by street-level bureaucrats, as Lipsky argued decades ago (1980).

My intention is not to idealize such contestations or struggles, but simply to redirect our attention. Struggles over care need to be identified and illuminated. We witness such struggles within families, between families and care authorities, between family caregivers and professionals as well as between professional groups. We also witness struggles within municipalities, nation states, the EU, and in international organizations like the ILO. These are struggles about the ideals of care, financing of care, and of the rights of those who provide and receive care. These struggles are related to the intense transformations taking place within elderly care and to the fact that care has become a political concern. However, we cannot view these struggles as creating dilemmas between immanent rationalities, as I will discuss later in this book. Rather, we must identify the logics at play, the potential of struggles between different logics and the potential of resistance to developments and regulation.

Struggles in Elderly Care

Interdependency or interrelatedness between people is one of the main characteristics of care. Care is about vulnerability (Fineman 2008), about the relatedness between individuals and between individuals and the community when we are not healthy, not productive and not autonomous individuals. In Chap. 3, I will expand on some additional characteristics of care in a contemporary context. When I use the terminology 'those [...] receiving care' above, it does not mean that the world is inhabited by two groups of people: those providing and those receiving care. Identities are not that clear-cut. Instead, people are interdependent (Tronto 1993), that is, able to give and receive care simultaneously. Or to paraphrase the Danish philosopher Lars-Henrik Schmidt, we are all disabled in some sense, and thereby in need of care at some time or another (Schmidt 1995).

This multitude of care can make it difficult to pin down what 'care' actually is. Some argue that care in itself is a mystery, that it is difficult—if not impossible—to understand or describe (Joanna Latimer, quoted in a discussion among researchers by Ceci et al. 2012). In my view, care is neither a mystery nor a simple action or sequence of thinking, action and emotion. We cannot understand *care as such*, since care takes place in many forms, institutional settings, and national contexts and under the influence of various global discourses. Hence, a theoretical model for understanding struggles about care must be grounded in a specific form of care. We cannot describe care in general terms but must relate to the specific field and its logics, as the Dutch philosopher Annemarie Mol argues (2008). Only in so doing can we understand the specific features of the contestations and struggles in the field. In this book, the specific field is paid elderly care. It therefore requires a context-sensitive concept of care. Focus on a specific type of care does not preclude us from thinking about the analytical vocabulary of care. As I argue in Chap. 3, we need to rethink care in a more general sense, using the insights from more specific studies.

This book relies on my own research—a case study—and that of others. I have studied the discursive regulation of elderly care in Denmark from the 1950s to 2015, conducted focus group interviews and observations in various municipalities on the translation, resistance and lived effects of this regulation from 2006 onwards (Dahl 2000a, 2009; Dahl et al. 2015b). This is a case study on the Danish political-administrative regulation of elderly care at two levels: the national and in different municipalities. The case study consists of several interrelated research projects during the last two decades in Denmark. The examples used are from my research projects and their focal points, as well as heuristic examples where theoretical concepts are illustrated through the use of pedagogical examples. Occasionally, I will refer to examples from other fields of care. My examples serve to illustrate sociopolitical develop-ments within elderly care, with the goal of mapping out the elderly care landscape and its struggles. The examples are primarily from the Nordic countries, although I also include some examples from other European countries. The map shows the terrain for struggles about elderly care in Nordic countries. This kind of map might soon become relevant for other European countries, inasmuch as the Nordic countries have often been considered as front runners in the field of elderly care and thereby inspired other countries. This observation does not mean that I construct the Nordic model of elderly care as *the* model of good elderly care. On the contrary, my goal has been to theorize care by sensitizing it to space and time, and *not* to simply assemble material on similarities and dif-ferences between the Nordic countries on elderly care. My mission in this book, using examples and case studies, is to draw context-sensitive insights on power, resistance and struggles.

A Map of Struggles

In order to understand the increasing proliferation of struggles about elderly care, we need a map.[6] A map can inform us about where we are and the topography of the terrain. Such a map may not be pre-cise concerning specificities, but it can help us get a sense of what is going on. The map tries to chart the main kinds of struggles that take place—and the seven processes mentioned previously that form the terrain of the field. It is not an exhaustive map, as it will also exhibit white spots—the terrain that has not yet been investigated. But it is a map that reveals the principal characteristics of the terrain—social and political processes as well as the main sites of struggles. The map is provisional and, like this book, gives us one—possible—answer to the questions: *What kinds of struggles are we witnessing?*

One can imagine infinite ways of identifying—and categorizing—dif-ferent kinds of struggles about care. Analysts using competing, norma-tive theoretical frameworks would view struggles in terms of justice, or ethics or even democracy. Such frameworks are advocated by the American philosopher Nancy Fraser (2008), the American psychologist Gilligan (1982) and the American political theorist Joan Tronto (1993, 2013). Fraser takes her point of departure in theories of justice (2008), Gilligan understands care as immersed in an ethic of care (1982), while Tronto has now positioned discussions about care on the terrain of democracy (Tronto 2013). None of these frameworks will be used here. Rather, I offer a more grounded approach, and I do not *a priori* define whether the struggles concern justice, ethics or democracy. Instead, I study the struggles and consider the framings made by the agents themselves. The content of the struggles thereby becomes grounded in the agents' own understanding and the discourses available to them. This context-sensitive framework gives us a more bottom-up picture of the tensions and struggles supplementing the broader, more general theoretical frameworks.

In contemporary society, we can identify a multitude of struggles over the different forms of care—the institutional arrangements, national policies and different logics—and between different levels of governance. In order to map these struggles, I have simplified the map to two major kinds of struggles. These are either neglected in existing research or judged to being of prime importance in the future and thus a source of insights into struggles about care more generally. One kind of struggle refers to fights against silencing—of fights to retain a plurality of voices and not just one hegemonic one—in elderly care, while the second kind concerns the regulation of care—which is in effect, struggles between the different care logics and between the different levels of regulation. By 'regulation' of care I mean the politicization of care, state responsibility or not, the forms of governing care and the valorization accorded to the various elements of care.

There are also some struggles about care that are not included in the book. Struggles over caring obligations—and negotiations—that take place *exclusively* within families—and between family members—are not discussed. Nor are struggles about who is included in the caring community (the in- or exclusion of particular groups from care in a globalizing world of increasingly nomadic subjects). For example, I do not deal with the issue of whether the partner of the migrant care professional, her parents and her children are also included in the new, national caring community. This would require another book, one that would describe the interplay between migrating regimes, the politics of belonging and care. A third blank spot of this map concerns the struggles between professional carers' groups over occupational boundaries. These are struggles about issues such as: Who should do what for those in need of care? Who should take responsibility for which elderly and which caring needs? The three types of struggle, which I will not deal with in this book, are all important, not least for the elderly as they pose the existential question of who will care for me—and in what way. Although these three forms of struggles are important and mentioned in this book, they are not at the core of my attention. Hence, instead of making a rather superficial and exhaustive map, I have chosen instead to focus on two kinds of struggles—those about silencing and those over regulation—which I believe are neglected and typical of the struggles currently taking place.

Struggles About Silencing and Regulation

Struggles over silencing are struggles to gain visibility. It is about leaving a space that has been hidden from view, silenced, and entering the public sphere of contestations in order to bring a set of care issues into the political agenda. Struggling against a process of silencing takes place alongside the spoken and without an intentional agent (Dahl 2012a). Alternatively, the struggle against silencing can be directed at certain features or practices of care. These are not always easy processes to identify, as they are sometimes *prior* to 'the politics of need interpretation' (Fraser 1989), where the focus is on the struggles about the needs themselves. Let me provide an example where the state has been silencing elements of care. Prior to 1968, 'loneliness' was part of the political discourse about elderly care in Denmark. By 'political discourse' I refer to the way politicians think and talk about the responsibilities of the state toward the elderly. In their horizon, home helps should have 'time to talk with the elderly' and to enable 'coziness'. Conversation over a cup of coffee was seen to help relieve the loneliness of the elderly. However, after 1968 'loneliness' and 'coziness' and its accompanying needs disappeared from the discourse. These themes were silenced and forgotten in the political-administrative discourse—no longer were they mentioned as needs (Dahl 2000). Home helps were no longer supposed to view their job tasks as including that of relieving 'loneliness'. There was a retrenchment of the state, a hollowing out of care, where state responsibility for 'loneliness' was reduced. Other needs were deemed more pressing, or perhaps as more manageable in terms of performance measurements, were viewed as more pressing. I will return to this example of the silencing of loneliness in Chap. 4 where I will also expand on the theoretical backdrop to silencing.

The second kind of struggle concerns how care should be talked about and acted upon within politics and the political. These are struggles about the regulation of care. One way to understand such struggles is to focus exclusively on politics as we conventionally know it, the authoritative allocation of values and who gets what, when and how (Laswell 1950). This is an important definition of politics but insufficient in its narrow understanding. So much will be excluded if we don't see the conflicts and struggles arising in the social before they get included in the formal sphere of politics. Therefore I will take another road. I will focus on the political as defined earlier in a more inclusive way and not limit the political to the formal political sphere, and I will see regulation as inspired by governmentality, a concept coined by Foucault. Governmentality can be interpreted and used in various ways. I am inspired by Foucault and the way 'governmentality' has been interpreted as identifying different 'governmentalities'. Mentalities involve 'particular representations, knowledges and often expertise regarding that which is to be governed' (Larner and Walters 2004: 2).[7] This combination of regulation and knowledge is aptly phrased in the quotation: 'To *govern* it is necessary to *know*' (Rose 2000: 209, quoted after Bacchi 2009: 11). I engage with the literature on governmentality and the new logics that are identified in contemporary forms of thinking and regulating care.[8] As Foucault could not have foreseen developments in governmentality and the way it has moved outside the nation state container, I will supplement governmentality with yet another dimension concerning struggles, namely their 'levels of governance'. By 'levels of governance' I refer to the different levels of the state, such that struggles can occur at the sub-national, national, intergovernmental (transnationally) and/or supranational levels. This becomes multilevel governmentality, a concept about which I will elaborate later in Chap. 5. I will try to highlight the different levels of struggles as they take place, but as the aim is to develop our theorization of struggles about care, a systematic multilevel analysis will not be applied.

In restricting my focus to two kinds of struggles, they should not be seen as exhaustive descriptions. Our map will contain, as I have explained, some blank spots. The blank spots not covered here comprise the struggles between groups of care professionals or care workers, struggles between relatives, and struggles about who is included in the community of care. While these struggles are also important, I believe that the two chosen struggles are strongly related to the spots not covered. Additionally other researchers have dealt with the struggles between professionals such as in the sociology of professions.

A Feminist, Critical Insider

A map like the one to be constructed here is produced at a specific point in time and in a specific context by a specific person. The map reflects my own situated knowledge. A long time ago, Haraway reminded us that all knowledge is situated, and that we are deemed to think through localities (Haraway 1988). My own position is that of a critical insider in a Nordic welfare regime: seeing and analyzing the world from a particular geographical and historical perspective and from a specific feminist position inspired by post-structuralism and radical feminism (Dahl 2010, 2012b). Let me briefly explain this position in order to facilitate a better understanding of the premises, understandings and arguments that I will present in this book.

Being born and raised in a Nordic country at the geographical intersection between Denmark and Germany that is, between the Nordic countries and Europe, has given me a historical experience of states as different. That some states are not *a priori* patriarchal, but can be seen as 'potentially women friendly' (Hernes 1987). These states can also possibly be seen as visionary on some gender issues (Carlsson 2014), and of the differences between different states in regard to feminist issues. This does not mean that the Nordic welfare states are the embodiment of some kind of feminist paradise. Much of my work has been to deconstruct this image and elucidate some of the less flattering elements of the Nordic welfare states, for example the misrecognition of care (Dahl 2004, 2010). However, the Nordic welfare states have taken on a public responsibility for elderly care relatively early and have to some extent (although timing and extent differs) engineered care professions. In this context, it should be noted that 'the state' is not a homogenous entity, but an ensemble of forces, discourses and strategies that must be identified and analyzed (Brown 1992; Pringle and Watson 2004; Kantola and Dahl 2005). We can identify struggles within the state about care and struggles between different levels for example, sub-national and the national; I shall on this elaborate later.

My feminist position is a post-structuralist one in that I focus attention on discourses, struggles while trying to avoid reproducing dichotomies (Derrida 1976, 1981; Flax 1990). One dichotomy often used is that between care and governance. Care becomes idealized, whereas governance becomes demonized. This is an untenable position in a modern, capitalist system, where even the most intimate types of care are commodified, managed and governed by a neo-liberal state. Various explanations for the intervention of the state in the management and governance of care can be listed, among them controlling expenses, ensuring the quality of care and ensuring a just distribution of care and equality in the caregiving practices. When labeling myself a radical feminist, I refer to the emotional, intangible and non-economic aspects of any gendered system (Jonasdottir 1991) such as those also involved in the practices of care. For me, this means being attentive to the ways in which discourses express—or fail to express—emotional elements of care. Regardless of whether emotional elements are sought disciplined explicitly, implicitly or silenced, they are part of an emotional regime, an issue to which I will return later in this book. Another dichotomy concerns gender, which lies at the core of feminist research. Here, however, I am not studying gendered subject positions for example, masculinities and femininities. Societal processes of gendering and de-gendering are important, and they alter the conditions of possibility for care, as will be shown in Chap. 2. Instead, I will focus on gendered regulation by investigating how gendered dichotomies are deeply ingrained in regulation and especially in the regulation of care (more about this in Chap. 5). I am not so much concerned about the 'who' of regulation but about how gendered regulation is played out in the policy sphere, and potentially resisted.

As a gender researcher, I place strong emphasis on an interdisciplinary approach; thus, I draw on (feminist) sociology, (feminist) political science, nursing philosophy and feminist history. Feminist sociology has been a driving force in the theorization of care. Unfortunately, this has brought with it a sociological bias that has tended to squeeze out potential contributions from other disciplines. Being strongly convinced that theorization of care is an interdisciplinary enterprise, we need to restrain the sociological bias and integrate insights from political science. We need to focus on power, struggles and regulation of care. As the political—and political-theoretical—understanding of care is weak, as also argued by Hannah-Kaisa Hoppania (2015), I suggest that we integrate into our approach a broad Foucault-inspired notion of power, struggles, resistance and the state (Foucault 1978, 1979). In order to illustrate this sociological bias and some of its weaknesses, I will present a summary of the various research traditions in care in Chap. 3.

Why Is This Book Necessary?

Feminist theorizing on care developed out of the feminist movement's attempt to insert a social activity, that is, care, onto the scientific agenda. By naming 'care', it was no longer hidden from the scientific (and traditionally male) gaze. Feminist care theory has contributed with important concepts such as 'a labor of love', 'rationality of care' (Wærness 1987), 'professional carers' (Davies 1995), 'privileged irresponsibility' (Tronto 1993), 'circles of care' (Bubeck 1995), 'global care chains' (Hochschild 2001), 'caring about the carer' (Kittay et al. 2005) and a 'logic of care' (Mol 2008)—to mention some of the key concepts. Feminist theorizing on care has successfully created a new field of research with new analytical concepts and a new perspective on social reality that moves us beyond a Marxist view of 'reproduction'. However, something is missing. The literature seems to have neglected or overlooked power and struggles *per se*, apart from some exceptions (Bubeck 1995; Dahl 2000b; Hockey and James 1993; Tronto 1993, 2010). Describing elderly care as a de-politicized field means ignoring the struggles between discourses about care, about the proper way to provide care, struggles between different professional groups about control or avoidance of care (or elements of care) and within the state about the regulation of care. The map provided in this book elucidates some of these struggles and their characteristics. In a sense, the map is a theoretical tool for analyzing the landscape of care and contemporary struggles over and about care.

The existing literature has not neglected struggles altogether. I will return to this issue in Chap. 3, where I discuss the task of theorizing care and power more thoroughly. Here I will just mention that the theorization of care has so far focused on the unequal distribution of care responsibilities from a gendered perspective in the early British, feminist theorization of care—burdens of care—and on the asymmetries of power that emerge in the infantilizing of the elderly (Hockey and James 1993). In my view, however, being attentive to power is not sufficient. Despite the important insights contributed by the theorization of care, the research field never considers struggles and resistance more systematically, nor do researchers theorize power in relation to the state and regulation. I am aware that making such broad statements about a field of research may seem hazardous, as it is difficult to do justice to such a multifaceted and varied field of research and theorizing as care, and care for elderly. However, painting with a big brush is sometimes necessary in order to understand the broader picture and to truly problematize the gaps in existing research on elderly care. In this light, let me now move on to an issue that goes beyond the hitherto national focus.

Struggles, Multilevel Governmentality and Transnational Discourses

Struggles about the silencing of care and the regulation of care take place in the political sphere and more broadly in the political. Politics no longer exclusively takes place in a national container (Fraser 2008). Politics is now conducted at several levels—local, national, transnational—and sometimes even simultaneously. Struggles about care can thus play out at different levels of governance—understood as different levels of regulation—and between these levels. Typically, four such levels are identified: sub-national, national level, supranational or intergovernmental and/or global. These four levels constitute a 'global governmentality'. They signal the emergence of a global system, although not in a totalizing way. Instead 'global governmentality' should be understood as a fuzzy collection of heterogeneous discourses and practices (Larner and Walters 2004). While 'global governmentality' is not a clear-cut analytical concept, it can be viewed as a fruitful approach for guiding empirical inquiry (Larner and Walters 2004).

In this book, I apply both a narrow and a broad understanding of politics and the political as mentioned earlier. I refer to different levels of regulation such as the local (struggles in the municipality), nation state, intergovernmental (primarily within the EU), supranational (EU) and transnational (OECD, WHO, OECD, ILO). Special attention is paid to how struggles have played out within the state as these are important for how much the state should care and in what way. The point of contention is about how much the state should 'care about care', that is, struggles along the traditional right-left distinction about the role of the state. On the other hand, there is contention about how the state carries out its caring: How does the state govern and frame issues of care, for example, as a 'care crisis', 'care burden', 'social investment' and/or as 'giving users a choice'? These issues concern how new governmentalities—or logics—are introduced. With every new logic, we need to identify what is being silenced, who is included or excluded, and how we are being governed. We need to investigate how states frame the issue of care, and what kinds of strategies they are pursuing. Moreover, we need to determine whether different parts of the state are framing key issues differently.

Whether different parts of the state frame elderly care differently becomes interesting to study in a context of states that see themselves as competitors in a global arena (Pedersen 2011), and when transnational discourses are originating in international knowledge regimes and traveling around the globe (Sahlin-Andersson 2002; Dahl et al. 2015a). Regulation of care is becoming transnational in the way that care becomes problematized in similar ways across the globe with identical buzzwords such as 'elderly burden', 'social investment', 'rehabilitation' and 'innovation'. Discourses, ideas and rationalities are traveling fast between countries (Bacchi 2009), as are the problems in transnational discourses (Conrad 2011). We witness transnational spaces of fluidity where actors and ideas circulate and are exchanged. The traveling discourses make it difficult to identify the different levels of governance involved. However, different levels of regulation have different jurisdictions and competencies. The EU, for example, manages its social affairs as part of the double subsidiarity, such that the EU cannot issue social affairs legislation, as this area is understood to be best governed by the individual member states and by families (Nousianen 2011). However, the more consultative, Open Method of Coordination (OMC), where key issues are discussed in a regular forum, is a new way of governing in politically sensitive areas that tries to tackle the diversity among member states. OMC endows new identities on participating civil servants and politicians, and provides new logics—ways of thinking—and new techniques for governance, such as 'best practice' in elderly care.

As the EU example shows, the new emerging global governmentality with its multilevel regulation changes the way the regulation of care is taking place. National discourses of elderly care are increasingly linked to transnational discourses and to debates, to 'learning processes', consultative forums and hegemonic discourses promoted by international organizations and conventions. Studying the regulation of elderly care also requires being attentive to the ways that international institutions exercise power in different ways.

The Structure of the Book

So far I have tried to document the increasing proliferation of struggles about elderly care through examples from Europe. In order to identify these struggles, we need to supplement existing perspectives with a political science perspective that investigates power, resistance, silencing, regulation and the global aspects of this regulation. I have outlined my position as a critical feminist insider, and my project is to draw a map of these struggles based on a Nordic context and on the transformations taking place in the regulation of care toward a global governmentality. This map is not exhaustive as it only includes the most crucial issues worth researching today. Perhaps in forthcoming research the blank spots can be studied and theorized.

In the second chapter, I focus on more historical and hermeneutic issues. I outline the seven main transformations that have created the background for changes in the way we, as social beings, think and act in relation to elderly care. Care becomes a site of struggle at the intersection of these seven social and political processes: commodifying, professionalizing, late modernizing, de-gendering, globalizing, bureaucratizing and the advent of neo-liberalism. The key question becomes: *In what way are key social and political processes changing the conditions of care, creating tensions and making care into a site of struggle?*

The third chapter deals with care as an analytical concept. I argue here that we need a radical rethinking of the care concept. I believe that earlier research on care has posed the wrong questions on the wrong theoretical terrain. Research has concerned itself with how to describe care and its main analytical dimensions on an exclusively ethical terrain. This line of inquiry has left us at an impasse as we cannot see power, silence, resistance and struggles—and struggles about regulation—in such a theoretical terrain. We therefore need to rephrase the question as: *How are the changing conditions of care and an attention to power and struggles reframing our theorizing about care?* I suggest that we theorize care as an assemblage of known others—families and friends—and strangers, by which we can reframe dilemmas into struggles between logics and become attentive to the emotional regime(s) currently at play.

The outline of a new analytical vocabulary of care is continued in the next two chapters. In the fourth chapter I focus on one kind of struggle in the current situation, that of silencing of care or elements of care and the struggles against silencing. Struggles about silence are about both dominance and subalternity (the latter understood as subordination). The chapter outlines the theoretical and philosophical backdrop to silencing, providing examples of struggles about visibility of care and the ideals of care. I outline three analytical strategies to identify processes of silencing: deconstruction, comparative discourse analysis and memory work. Silencing is in fact a de-politicizing of care. The main questions here become: *What characterizes struggles about silencing in care? And how can we identify silencing as a process in documents?*

I continue to elaborate the new analytic and vocabulary in the fifth chapter which is about a second kind of struggle, that of regulation. In general terms, these are struggles about the form and content of regulating elderly care, although the form/content distinction is difficult to uphold in empirical studies. The chapter describes the transformations in the regulation of elderly care, focusing on three main features: the hybridity of regulation, the multilevel governmentality and the gendered form of regulation. At the same time, these characteristics constitute the key sites of struggles about the regulation of care. The key questions to be answered in this chapter are: *How can we understand the regulation of care today? And what kind of struggles can we identify in the regulation of care?*

In the final chapter, we return to the key question of the book: *Which kinds of struggles can we identify?* The map of elderly care is described with the two different kinds of struggles as major focal points on the map and I elaborate the crucial differences between them. The potential implications of my analysis and analytic for other policy fields of care are discussed. A final section of the book raises the pressing issue of the necessity to govern care, and reflects on the current form of regulation and its potential negative effects. The issue is crucial in our current context where care and regulation are not seen in opposition to each other, and where they may be in fact moving beyond neo-liberalizing.

Notes

1. New Public Management (NPM) is a term originally coined by Christopher Hood (1991). NPM refers to the introduction of management ideas from private enterprise into the state. More on NPM in Chap. 5, that discusses the regulating of care.
2. This may also be the case with the broad category of 'Asian Values', something mentioned by Asian researchers studying care chains (Huang et al. 2012: 198).
3. Naturally logics are not struggling by themselves, but agents are seen as carriers of different logics which are potentially conflicting in their meetings.
4. A field of care has changeable boundaries in so far as understandings of what care is and who needs care change historically, which has already been pointed out by Finch (1989).

5. There exist different discourses and when I later write that 'discourses compete' this is shorthand for a situation where different agents use various discourses. Discourses cannot exist independently of their use—reproduction—by agents.

6. A similar concept and use of the 'map' can be found in the writings of Nancy Fraser (2008), but the 'map' has a longer history dating back to the philosophy of science (Toulmin 1952), using different theorizations as (temporary) instruments. Also Bröckling et al. (2010: 16) have recently used a concept of local 'cartography' similar to that of a 'map'.

7. The concept of 'mentalities' is in my understanding a synonym for 'logic', so when I use 'logics' I refer to both rationalities as in Mol's understanding, and to mentalities as in Foucault's understanding.

8. I also engage with the literature on New Public Management, reforms and care, and I study the ways in which this new form of governance is producing and changing care.

References

Arendt, H. (1958). *The human condition*. Chicago: University of Chicago Press.

Bacchi, C. (2009). *Analysing policy: What's the problem represented to be?* Frenchs Forest: Pearson Education.

Bröckling, U., Krasmann, S., & Lemke, T. (2010). From Foucault's lectures at the Collège de France to studies of governmentality—An introduction. In U. Bröckling, S. Krasmann, & T. Lemke (Eds.), *Governmentality—Current issues and future challenges* (pp. 1–33). London: Routledge.

Brown, W. (1992). Finding the man in the state. *Feminist Studies, 18*(1), 7–34.

Bubeck, D. (1995). *Care, gender and justice*. Oxford: Clarendon Press.

Carlsson, K. (2014). *Den tilfällige husmodern*. Lund: Nordic Academic Press.

Ceci, C., Björnsdottir, K., & Purkis, M. E. (2012). Introduction: Home, care, practice—Changing perspectives on care at home for older people. In C. Ceci, K. Björnsdottir, & M. E. Purkis (Eds.), *Perspectives on care at home for older people* (pp. 1–22). London: Routledge.

Conrad, C. (2011). Social policy history after the transnational turn. In P. Kettunen & K. Petersen (Eds.), *Beyond welfare state models* (pp. 218–240). Cheltenham: Edward Elgar.

Dahl, H. M. (2000a). *Fra kitler til eget tøj—Diskurser om professionalisme, omsorg og køn, Ph.D. thesis*. Aarhus: Politica, Aarhus university.

Dahl, H. M. (2000b). A perceptive and reflective state? *The European Journal of Women's Studies, 7*(4), 475–494.

Dahl, H. M. (2004). A view from the inside: Recognition and redistribution in the Nordic welfare state from a gender perspective. *Acta Sociologica, 47*(4), 325–337.

Dahl, H. M. (2009). New public management, care and struggles about recognition. *Critical Social Policy, 29*(4), 634–654.

Dahl, H. M. (2010). An old map of state feminism and an insufficient recognition of care. *NORA—Nordic Journal of Feminist and Gender Research, 18*(3), 152–166.

Dahl, H. M. (2012a). Tavshed som magt og afmagt. *Tidsskriftet Antropologi, 33*(66), 3–16.

Dahl, H. M. (2012b). Neo-liberalism meets the Nordic welfare state—Gaps and silences. *NORA, 20*(4), 283–288.

Dahl, H. M., Hansen, A. E., Hansen, C. S., & Kristensen, J. E. (2015a). *Kamp og status—De lange linjer i børnehaveinstitutionens og pædagogprofessionens historie fra 1820 til 2015*. Copenhagen: U Press.

Dahl, H. M., Eskelinen, L., & Hansen, E. B. (2015b). Coexisting principles and logics of elder care: Help to self-help and consumer-oriented service. *International Journal of Social Welfare, 24*(3), 287–295.

Davies, C. (1995). Competence versus care? Gender and caring work revisited. *Acta Sociologica, 38*(1), 17–31.

Derrida, J. (1976). *Of grammatology* (G. Chakravorty Spivak, Trans.). Baltimore: Johns Hopkins University Press.

Derrida, J. (1981). *Disseminations* (B. Johnson, Trans.). Chicago: The University of Chicago Press.

Finch, J. (1989). *Family obligations and social change*. Cambridge: Polity.

Fineman, M. (2008). The vulnerable subject: Anchoring equality in the human condition. *Yale Journal of Law and Feminism, 21*(1), 1–24.

Flax, J. (1990). *Thinking fragments*. Berkeley: University of California Press.

Foucault, M. (1978). *The history of sexuality—An introduction*. London: Penguin Books.

Foucault, M. (1979). *Discipline and punish –The birth of the prison*. London: Penguin Books.

Fraser, N. (1989). Talking about needs: Interpretive contests as political conflicts in welfare state societies. *Ethics, 99*, 291–313.

Fraser, N. (2008). *Scales of justice—Reimagining political space in a globalizing world*. Cambridge: Polity.

Gilligan, C. (1982). *In a different voice*. Cambridge, MA: Harvard University Press.

Haraway, D. (1988). Situated knowledges: The science question in feminism and the privilege of perspective. *Feminist Studies, 14*(3), 575–599.

Hernes, H. (1987). *Welfare state and woman power—Essays in state feminism.* Oslo: Universitetsforlaget.

Hochschild, A. R. (2001). Global care chains and emotional surplus value. In W. Hutton & A. Giddens (Eds.), *On the edge: Living with global capitalism* (pp. 130–146). London: Vintage.

Hockey, J., & James, A. (1993). *Growing up and growing old—Ageing and dependency in the life course.* London: SAGE.

Hood, C. (1991). A public management for all seasons? *Public Administration, 69*(1), 3–19.

Hoppania, H. (2015). *Care as a site of political struggle.* Ph.D. thesis, Helsinki: University of Helsinki, Department of Political and Economic Studies.

Hoppania, H., & Vaittinen, T. (2015). A household full of bodies: Neoliberalism, care and 'the political'. *Global Society, 29*(1), 70–88.

Huang, S., Yeoh, B. S. A., & Toyota, M. (2012). Caring for the elderly: The embodied labour of migrant care workers in Singapore. *Global Networks, 12*(2), 195–215.

Isaksen, L. W. (2011). Gendering the stranger: Nomadic care workers in Europe—A Polish-Italian example. In H. M. Dahl, M. Keränen, & A. Kovalainen (Eds.), *Europeanization, care and gender—Global complexities* (pp. 141–151). Basingstoke: Palgrave Macmillan.

Jacobs, A, & Century, A. (2012, September 7). Duty first, in an ageing China. *International Herald Tribune*, p. 2.

Johansson, S. (1994). Omöblering i folkhemmet. Nytt vin i gamla läglar? In L. Simonen (Ed.), *När gränserna flyter—en nordisk antologi om vård och omsorg* (pp. 31–50). Jyväskylä: STAKES.

Jonasdottir, A. (1991). *Love power and political interests.* Örebro/Kumla: University of Örebro/Kumla tryckeri.

Kantola, J., & Dahl, H. M. (2005). Gender and the state: From differences between to differences within. *International Journal of Feminist Politics, 7*(1), 49–70.

Kittay, E. F., Jennings, B., & Wasunna, A. A. (2005). Dependency, difference and the global ethic of long-term care. *The Journal of Political Philosophy, 13*(4), 443–469.

Larner, W., & Walters, W. (2004). Introduction—Global governmentality: Governing international spaces. In W. Larner & W. Walters (Eds.), *Global governmentality—Governing international spaces* (pp. 1–20). London: Routledge.

Laswell, H. D. (1950). *Politics: Who gets what, when and how.* New York: Peter Smith.

Lipsky, M. (1980). *Street-level bureaucracy.* New York: Russell Sage Foundation.

Lloyd, L. (2006). Call us carers: Limitations and risks in campaigning for recognition and exclusivity. *Critical Social Policy, 26*(4), 945–960.

Mol, A. (2008). *The logic of care—Health and the problem of patient choice.* Oxon: Routledge.

Mouffe, C. (2005). *On the political.* London: Routledge.

Newman, J., & Tonkens, E. (2011). Introduction. In J. Newman & E. Tonkens (Eds.), *Participation, responsibility and choice* (pp. 9–28). Amsterdam: Amsterdam University Press.

Norval, A. (1996). *Deconstructing apartheid discourse.* London: Verso.

Nousianen, K. (2011). Double subsidiarity, double trouble? Allocating care responsibilities in the EU through social dialogue. In H. M. Dahl, M. Keränen, & A. Kovalainen (Eds.), *Europeanization, care and gender— Global complexities* (pp. 21–40). Basingstoke: Palgrave Macmillan.

Pedersen, O. K. (2011). *Konkurrencestaten.* Copenhagen: Hans Reitzels forlag.

Pringle, R., & Watson, S. (2004). Women's interests and the post-structuralist state. In A. Phillips (Ed.), *Feminism and politics* (pp. 203–223). Oxford: Oxford University Press.

Rasmussen, L. D. (2012). *(H)vide verden—om relationer mellem professionsidentiteter og kvalitetssikring, Ph.D. thesis.* Roskilde: Department of Society and Globalisation, Roskilde University.

Rose, N. (2000). *Powers of freedom: Reframing political thought.* Cambridge: Cambridge University Press.

Sahlin-Andersson, K. (2002). National, international and transnational constructions of new public management. In T. Christensen & P. Lægreid (Eds.), *The transformation of ideas and practice* (pp. 43–72). Aldershot: Ashgate.

Schmidt, L. H. (1995, August). Velfærd til forhandling. *Social forskning,* pp. 99–107.

Stone, D. (2000). Caring by the book. In M. H. Meyer (Ed.), *Care work, gender, labour and the welfare state* (pp. 89–111). London: Routledge.

Toulmin, S. (1952). *The philosophy of science.* London: Hutchinson.

Tronto, J. (1993). *Moral boundaries.* New York: Routledge.

Tronto, J. (2010). Creating caring institutions: Politics, plurality and purpose. *Ethics & Social Welfare, 4*(2), 158–171.

Tronto, J. (2013). *Caring democracy—Markets, equality and justice.* New York: New York University Press.

Vabø, M., & Szebehely, M. (2012). A caring state for all older people? In A. Anttonen, L. Häikiö, & K. Stefánsson (Eds.), *Welfare state, universalism and diversity* (pp. 121–143). Cheltenham: Edward Elgar.

Wærness, K. (1987). On the rationality of caring. In A. Showstack-Sassoon (Ed.), *Women and the state* (pp. 207–234). London: Hutchinson.

Weber, M. (1921). *Wirtschaft und gesellschaft.* Tübingen: J.C.B. Mohr.

Williams, F. (2010, July 8–11). *Claiming and framing in the making of care politics: The recognition and redistribution of care.* Paper presented at the 5th International Carers Conference: New Frontiers in Caring, Leeds.

2

The Changing Landscape of Elderly Care and the Proliferation of Struggles

The stories we tell matter. Stories create a coherent understanding about the past, the present and the future. However, we should be cautious about the stories we tell, both as feminists and as social scientists. We tend to create stories of progress or loss, and we often gloss over the varied, complex and perhaps contradictory voices of the past and the present. This makes our narratives more homogenous (Hemmings 2011) silencing some elements. Such warnings are not altogether new. The sociologist Janet Finch (1989), in her study of the history of caring obligations, warned us against constructing an image of a golden, all-caring society in the past. The story I am going to tell is more complex than a story about a (global) care crisis (Hochschild 1995; Saraceno 1997; Isaksen et al. 2008) or of an 'impending eldercare crisis' (Huang 2012). It is not exclusively a story of loss (care crisis).

Many changes have affected the current state of care. Various social and political processes are interwoven with or directly impacting forms of care in positive and negative ways. Some of these changes have been ongoing for more than a century, for example, the professionalizing of caregivers; while other changes, such as neo-liberalizing, have taken place more recently. Whereas some theorists are concerned about the problem

© The Author(s) 2017
H.M. Dahl, *Struggles In (Elderly) Care*,
DOI 10.1057/978-1-137-57761-0_2

of care and the solutions to this situation (Tronto 2013), my concern is to understand the complexity of the current situation. This is not meant to be any kind of *Zeitdiagnose*, but rather, a more humble, hermeneutic aspiration to identify how things came to be this way, and the main features of the current situation as viewed from a critical, feminist position. Hence, the goal of this chapter is to contextualize the discussion about elderly care. I do this by identifying the processes at play, describing their logics, and discussing their complexity and some of their intersections with each other.

The reality of care is more complex than using a simple eschatology with a label of crisis as a metaphor for its transformation and conditions. Nevertheless, researchers agree that the ideologies and practices of care have changed profoundly over the last half a century. Whereas some researchers characterize this transformation as a revolution in care (Tronto 2013: 2), others focus on the general state of an unease between care and the world. Hence, the Australian sociologist Michael Fine observes that: 'Care is an essential feature of the social world, yet it no longer fits into the contemporary world in the way that it has in the past' (Fine 2007: 1).

Something concerning care has changed. Uneasiness has entered the scene. This uneasiness has created the background for a tension and a basis for struggles. In this chapter, we will identify these changes and their effects on care and elderly care struggles. The main question in this chapter is therefore: *What kind of social and political processes are changing the conditions of care, creating tensions and care as a site of struggle?*

Social and Political Processes Changing the Landscape

I can only attempt to identify some of the major societal and political processes that have created the new terrain and the conditions for care to become a site of struggle. I will provide a map that is useful in the current situation, focusing on the most important factors. Processes indicate change—and change creates uncertainties where individuals have to rethink themselves and their situation. It is these new uncertainties that can create resistance. Many social and political processes can be identified, and this process of identification always has a specific vantage point. My vantage point is that of a critical, feminist insider operating from within the so-called 'Nordic model'. As mentioned in the Introduction, I have mapped seven processes that are important for the terrain of care in general, and for elderly care in particular. Other scholars have identified fewer processes. Fine, for example, identifies four of them: occupational specialization, (postwar) welfare state, feminism and globalization (2007: 6–7). Fine's four processes are important, but they are also too general in relation to the state and to processes of occupational specialization to be useful, as I will explain below.

Therefore, I have identified the following seven processes that have fed into struggles about care: *commodifying, professionalizing, late modernizing, de-gendering, globalizing, bureaucratizing and neo-liberalizing*. Instead of occupational specialization as Fine (2007) mentions, I divide this into two processes, that of commodifying and professionalizing, as they are analytically and empirically different from each other, although clearly related. Instead of the welfare state, I distinguish between two processes: bureaucratizing and neo-liberalizing, as I believe that these, too, need to be kept analytically distinct. Bureaucratizing concerns documentation, general rules and impartiality, whereas neo-liberalizing refers to choices, marketization and self-management. These seven processes are still ongoing, and my list is not exhaustive. They are general processes that are not specific to elderly care, although they meet the field of elderly care in a specific way.[1] They are not to be seen as inevitable processes, but as processes mediated and translated by agency. Instead of nouns, I therefore use verbs to indicate that they are political processes and not deterministic. Sometimes they are supported and reproduced, sometimes they are resisted by agents. The relationship between the processes and care is in this sense intertwined. This is why I have made the nouns more 'active', for example, from 'neo-liberalism' to 'neo-liberalizing'. Specifying processes runs the risk of being immersed in each particular process. We risk overlooking the bigger picture of their interaction. The processes I describe here can overlap, contradict or reinforce each other. At the end of this chapter, I will try to specify briefly some examples of these varying kinds of relationships.

It is clear that additional societal and political processes affecting care could have been listed. However, my intention is not to create a complete map. Processes such as the use of new welfare technologies or the processes of racializing (Gavanas 2013) have not been included in my book. This is not because they are unimportant, but simply because not much research exists on these processes. In this chapter, I can only tentatively describe the changes occurring in the social and political realities and the very general way these changes have reconfigured the conditions for providing elderly care, identities, ideals of this care and care relations. Whereas the seven social and political processes are often described in a general way I have tried to think the topic of care and the vulnerable elderly into these processes of change. Change can create uncertainty, tensions between the old and the new logics, tensions within these processes, and resistance and tensions between the various elements of change, such as between the various seven societal processes. Let me begin this review with the first of these societal and political changes: commodifying care.

Commodifying Care: Markets, Outsourcing and Emotional Labor

One of the social and political processes shaping care is capitalism, understood as a form of production where labor is commodified. Care is labor, and care labor is sold on a market and not used for immediate consumption according to Karl Marx (Jessop 2008). The *raison d' être* of a market is to create a surplus, through what in Marxist terms is an exploitation of the care worker/care professional. Care as a form of labor is no longer solely performed by relatives, significant others and/or community members as unpaid care. Instead, a commodification of care takes place, which is simultaneously a marketization of intimacy (Ungerson 1997).[2] Strangers are paid for their care labor.[3] This changes care from being predominantly unpaid, based on an ethic/sense of belonging/labor of love, to a paid transaction between potential strangers. The caregiver is thus a care worker or care professional, employed by a firm, a Non-Profit Organization (NPO), the state, or directly by the elderly person.

When the institutional context of care changes care, the ideal(s) of care often change as well. However, this does not mean that emotions and the affective regime[4] are suspended *en toto when care becomes commodified*. It means, rather that the affective regime changes. These changes in an affective regime bind people together and create different affective regimes in commodified care: the regime creates affect for example, attachment and sympathy, as well as detachment and disgust in care. Different kinds of affects are, respectively, judged positively or negatively by society. The affective regime both 'aligns some subjects with others' (Ahmed 2004: 17) and positions some outside such an alignment. Some subjects align with others in those cases where care professionals feel closer to some elderly than others. Some elderly can be positioned outside such an alignment when the disorder or hygiene of their private home infuses embarrassment or disgust between the elderly and the care professional, thereby contributing to a regime of affective detachment.

Under capitalism, paying for care—by the recipient, family members, a company or the state—changes our relatedness to each other. Commodifying care has various implications. One refers to the macro-level of social systems; thus, the American philosopher Nancy Fraser (2011) argues that commodifying care impairs our capacities for sociocultural reproduction. In this way, Fraser says, commodifying itself leads to a care crisis. Another implication of capitalism and its transformation is the changing demands on its workers. Care companies and states are increasingly demanding more—and something different—of their workers and professionals. Across occupations and professions, Arlie R. Hochschild has identified an increasing focus on the proper emotions and their management, that is, what can be labeled a market for 'emotional labor' across occupations. Emotional labor 'requires one to induce or suppress feeling in order to sustain the outward countenance that produces the proper state of mind in others' (Hochschild 1983: 7). Hochschild operates with the assumption of an authentic self that is endangered by the emotional work required, leading to a less authentic self and a strain on the personality. Michael Hardt has defined affective labor as: 'production and manipulation of affects, [which] requires (virtual or actual) human contact and proximity' (Hardt 1999: 97–98). Hardt thereby expands the emotional work (the affects) to the simultaneous stress on information, communication and knowledge. And he expands the concept of affective labor to include 'virtual' human contact. In elderly care, this contact could take the form of human interaction via the computer, that is, telecare. Capitalism is ever more dependent upon emotional labor and is thereby potentially creating a strain between the 'real' feelings and the 'managed emotions' of the care worker/professional carer.

Nowadays many states pursue marketization strategies, hiring companies to provide care services under state contracts. Transnational companies have now entered the elderly care market and are making profits (Meagher and Szebehely 2013). In other cases, states are transferring cash subsidies to families who can use the subsidy as compensation for an income loss or hire a care worker to perform care in the family, as in Italy. Clare Ungerson has identified a typology of payments, ranging from carer allowances, proper wages, routed wages—through the care user, symbolic payment and paid volunteering (Ungerson 1997). We are dealing with a multifaceted development of capitalism with three main dimensions: *an extension of markets, a new logic of marketization within the state, as well as capitalism changing its form and integrating more affectual and communicative elements.*

Care has changed from being predominantly unpaid to being commodified and performed primarily by strangers. Markets for elderly care expand as a response to unmet care needs (or states outsourcing), and care workers or professional carers can either be employed in for-profit or non-profit organizations with presumably different organizational logics. In most welfare states, elderly care is becoming part of a booming market, and even in the more social-democratic welfare states, the markets for elderly care are expanding. Here state strategies inspired by New Public Management (NPM) are increasingly creating care markets instead of the former state-provided care (Meagher and Szebehely 2013). State responsibility for care is retained. But the state no more 'produces' the care, as the care services are now outsourced to private or semi-private providers, or to the families themselves in the form of subsidies. Commodification and capitalism also change, transforming their demands for what counts as 'good work'.

The extension of markets for elderly care creates uncertainty over expectations, price and conditions of care work. In addition, the outsourcing process can create tensions and conflicts between the state, the providing company and the vulnerable elderly when the contract conditions or customer assessment is not met. Municipalities face the prospect of private care companies suddenly going bankrupt, which would suddenly leave no one to care for the elderly. Finally, the logic of capitalist efficiency and the state managing of emotional labor (and the appropriate responses of their employees) intensify the demands on the care worker or professional carer. Potential lines of conflict arise regarding the demands and the ideal of what constitutes adequate care. Hence, the three elements of the commodifying of care can all lead to uncertainty, conflicts between the different parts in the provision of elderly care, and struggles about what legitimately can be demanded from the care worker and the care professional. Now to another process strongly related to the commodifying of care: professionalizing.

Professionalizing and Struggles About Knowledge, Ideals of Care and Boundaries

Another change to care relates to care moving out of the home and becoming related to particular forms of knowledge (Hänsel 1992). This process is hardly new; it has been going on for centuries with the early hospitals and asylums. The movement of care out of the home tends to be related to two processes: commodification (as already described) and professionalization.[5] The two processes are analytically different, although professionalizing is strongly linked to commodification. Professionalizing takes place when '... producers of special services sought to constitute and control a market for their expertise' (Larsson 1977: xvii). In this sense, representatives of an occupation try to create an image of a particular knowledge (of care) that only they possess, for example, nursing knowledge. In this way, professionalizing processes are also about recognition, power and money, and strategies of professionalization are often pursued as strategies for achieving higher status. Processes of professionalization are about formalization of education, including training in work situations. The possession of a particular kind of knowledge is what Weber has termed a 'knowledge monopoly' (Weber 1976 [1921]). Others have added autonomy to the characteristics of a profession (Parsons 1964; Freidson 2001). Changing the carer from an amateur to a professional is considered beneficial in the understanding that the (proper) knowledge of sickness and aging can improve care. Let me provide an example: A professional carer will notice the early signs of type 2 diabetes thereby ensuring timely diagnosis, earlier intervention in the dietary habits and eventually reducing the frequency of thrombosis. However, professionalizing is typically about privileging a particular form of knowledge and, in so doing, glossing over forms of knowledge that relate to the person in need of care—the vulnerable body and the body with a sickness—knowledge of the particular person, his/her condition and forms of gendered, racialized and class-based forms of acting. In order to become, and to be seen as, professional, an occupation needs to stress its mastery of certain forms of knowledge, notably the theoretical and universal patterns of knowledge. This means that particular forms of knowledge related to both the body of the vulnerable person and the person doing the care are less valued and neglected, as feminist philosophy and sociology tells us (Martinsen 1994; Witz 1992). Professionalization thus entails that care becomes less tailored to the particular needs of the vulnerable person, as the priority of abstract forms of knowledge does not allow more experience-based knowledge to be valued and used. Professionalizing is thus a double-edged sword, in so far as it privileges certain forms of knowledge over others.

Professionalizing can also result in struggles between various professions and between classical, well-established professional groups and welfare professions, as is the case between doctors and nurses or between nurses and certified social and health assistants (the latter are a Danish variety of auxiliary nurses). Struggles occur in the professional field, over the most and least attractive parts of care. Struggles may occur when several professional groups struggle to ensure the most interesting and challenging elements of care work for elderly, for example, rehabilitation. Is it the nurse, the physiotherapist or the certified social and health assistant who should coach and train the elderly to enable them to do more by themselves? Here different professional groups struggle to create an image that qualifications and knowledge base are best suited to the task of rehabilitating the elderly. Other struggles are about avoiding those care tasks seen as 'dirty, dangerous and degrading' and to assign these tasks to the least privileged groups.

Professionalizing processes are often seen as bottom-up oriented actions of groups seeking to create an image of a profession. However, such processes can also be engineered by the state. Indeed, Michel Foucault argues that there is a mutual dependency between the state and professionals. The state needs their expertise in order to regulate and govern the population (Foucault 1991; Johnson 1995).[6] Welfare professionals become part of the technologies of power, helping the state to discipline citizens into orderly, healthy lives. Let me provide an example. Today some patients in some Danish hospitals are asked to consult a preventive nurse before their discharge from hospital. In this conversation, the nurse talks to and motivates the patient to try to reconsider their drinking and/or smoking habits—and ultimately to change it/them (Dahlager 2001). Professions make the health policy goals of the state their own (Larsen 2013). In this way, the—welfare—professions are also involved in operations of power, not just as knowledgeable experts, but also as part of the state and its caring and health regime. Under these conditions, relations between professionals and the elderly can become sites of contestation over different forms of knowledge and power. However, there also arise tensions between different professional groups, as professionalizing processes embody particular ideas of knowledge and of what constitutes 'good care', along with guarding boundaries to other professions or to groups in the process of professionalizing.

To sum up: professionalizing changes care by privileging certain forms of knowledge over others and by activating struggles about ideals of care and professional boundaries. The ideal of care can be imagined in different ways, for example, such as complementing care[7] versus reablement (rehabilitation) or as preventive care versus alleviating suffering. These different professional ideals and ideals of care are bound to create struggles. Let us now move on to late modernity and see how the advent of this era has altered the landscape of care.

Individualization, Late Modern Families and Changing Images of Old Age

The late modern age, or high modernity, is a process whereby individuals, families and images of old age change. Late modernity is often seen as being characterized by an extreme self-reflectivity, where the self is a continuous, reflexive project (Giddens 1991). Individuals are said to continually monitor their actions and to be faced with a myriad of life choices. However, late modernity is difficult to delimit in relation to some of the other processes that relate to transformations in care, for example, globalizing processes and neo-liberalizing. In Giddens' view, late modernity refers to changes taking place at several levels and their interface, that is, globalization and intimization (Giddens 1992). The increasing global flow of culture, technology and persons is linked closely with changing personal dispositions (Giddens 1991). Late modernity cannot be analyzed independently of globalizing processes, as it is a pivotal component of this change. The same can be said for neo-liberalizing. Neo-liberalizing as consumerism involves making choices, as in late modernity (Jones and Higgs 2010). Despite this reservation, I will now deal with late modernizing, freezing the processes of neo-liberalizing and globalizing for a moment.

Individuals change—and so do social institutions such as the family. Ways of having and being a family change—for example, co-habitation, single motherhood, same-sex couples and parents, 'bonus' children from a spouse's previous marriage, etc. With changes in the family, images and expectations of old age also change. The image of old age is a plural one, ranging from an extended working life to an 'active senior life' ('60 is the new 40'), to a retirement of leisure, from grand-parenting to late parenting, and from sheltered housing to beach-front retirement communities (Jones and Higgs 2010: 1515). Families are more diversified, and this is also the case for care in old age. Late modernity has a differential impact on society. In some parts of society, it is layering on pre-existing, traditional ways of seeing the world, whereas in others late modernity is the dominant norm. This is shown in the studies of informal carers by the British sociologist Susan Pickard (2010). Pickard shows that some families have a more traditional, fatalistic way of thinking about care and care obligations, whereas others reveal a more late modern discourse about choices and self-realization as carer. Care is not just something that one does or feels obliged to; it is sometimes actively chosen as a responsibility, or resisted in favor of some other life project (Pickard 2010: 484).

Families also change.[8] The increasing paid employment of especially middle-class women changes the way life is lived within families. Instead of a single breadwinner family, we now witness the predominance of the dual breadwinner model, where women like men, are breadwinners that is, take up paid work. Although women are now breadwinners, there are still expectations about them caring for children and their aging parents or parents-in-law. Children born in the 1980s and onward in Denmark have nearly all attended nurseries and kindergartens in their childhood related to their mothers' salaried employment (Dahl et al. 2015a). This institutionalization of preschool care seems to change the care qualifications students have when entering nursing schools. The Danish social scientist Tine Rask Eriksen (2008) has analyzed the caring qualifications of nursing students studying in 1987 and 2002, respectively. Based on questionnaires and interviews, Eriksen argues that nursing students, due to their changed socialization process, have different qualifications. Domestic work in the household has increasingly become visible, negotiated and delegated within the family as a result of the mother's paid work. Care work has become institutionalized in nurseries and kindergartens. This means that the nursing students, while they have better communicative abilities, have a less practical sense and experience of actually taking care of siblings. Eriksen concludes that there is either a loss of caring qualifications or, alternatively, a new late modern way of performing care (2008: 40). In another study of first year nursing school students, the Norwegian social scientists Karen Jensen and Bodil Tveit (2005) observe between a youth culture stressing individualization, intimacy and the search for meaning versus a nursing school culture emphasizing altruism. In contrast to Eriksen, Jensen and Tveit argue that this clash is modified, and that the training redirects the students toward the needs and concerns of others, and that some students have even experienced personal change (Jensen and Tveit 2005: 169). Whereas Jensen and Tveit are optimistic, Eriksen seems to be concerned about the caring qualifications related to the body. Eriksen is pessimistic about the declining ability of nurses to provide hands-on care, which could create tensions between the vulnerable elderly and those supposed to provide professional care.

Images of old age also change as part of late modernity. Old age used to be defined as something at the periphery of society, denoting the sick, passive, elderly person in need of care. Increasingly, old age is at the center of our concern, and not just in connection with issues of health. We witness a new paradigm of aging that foregrounds the active and healthy old person, an emphasis on the pleasant side of aging, where issues of dependency and loneliness are silenced (Dahl 2005). Old age is viewed devoid of disease and disability, and an ideal of successful aging is promoted (O'Rourke and Ceci 2013). This paradigm combines discourses on healthy aging, independent living, successful aging and agelessness (Jones and Higgs 2010: 1516). This new paradigm—and the reframing of care needs—offers the elderly the hope of regaining autonomy and prolonging a healthy life as long as possible. However, there is also a dark side to this emphasis on elderly people being pressured to remain healthy and continually active (Dahl 2012a). Being an active senior becomes a moral obligation rather than a choice.

Late modernity changes conditions of care in several ways. Late modernity is not a homogenous process. It makes its impact at a differential pace in different parts of society—and also in various ways in different parts of the world. Forms of living together are becoming more diversified and may potentially create tensions and struggles about care, as obligations to give care are pressured by less stable family arrangements. In addition, the institutionalization of preschool care means that care qualifications are increasingly learned in institutionalized settings from those who will later become care professionals or care workers. This could be the cause of tensions between those giving and those in need of care, as there could occur a lack of fit between expectations and the desired care qualifications. Further causes of tensions can stem from the reframing of care needs into this new image of old age. Elderly people are now morally obliged to be active, including actively trying to prevent disease and inactivity. This new ideal of care could cause resistance. Let us now move on to a social process that is a substantial part of late modernity, but requires its own independent analysis: gendering and de-gendering.

Gendering and De-gendering of Care

Feminism and the feminist social movement(s) have turned their attention to women's rights and equality, successfully redefining the boundaries of the field of politics by getting new issues onto the political agenda; issues such as violence against women (now: partnership violence) and equal pay. The feminist struggle has also included attempts to change the gendered division of care, the status of care (Fraser 2013), and gender identities more generally. Feminism has many faces, having appeared in many waves during the last centuries. Here I am not concerned with the vast research on the nature of feminism as a social movement (Dahlerup 1986). Instead, this section is concerned with the changes that feminism and other social forces have generated in relation to the gendering and de-gendering of care—and how they relate to the changing conditions of elderly care. I see gendering as a process with no fixity—in line with the Australian researchers Carol Bacchi and Joan Eveline, who see gendering: 'as an incomplete and partial process in which bodies and politics are always becoming meaningful' (Eveline and Bacchi 2005: 502).

De-gendering is the opposite process, where efforts are made to de-link gender from bodies with gendered signs. De-gendering is a process of setting more traditional feminities and masculinities free. There has generally been a push toward a 'de-gendering' (Connell 2011), but gendering is still taking place in late modernity. Changes and stability are found in various spheres and levels of society. This again makes more likely the existence of discord and insecurity that can create tensions and clashes between different ways of understanding a given situation.

The above points to a societal change from below, but policies of gender equality have also been engineering changes in masculinity and femininity from above. Many nation states as well as the EU have implemented different forms of equality policies in various combinations, such as quotas, parental leave and gender mainstreaming policies. In this sense, gender issues have become part of politics and are now part of a global political agenda (Squires 2007). Generally, feminism has stressed the autonomy and the rights of women over their mind and body, and as a result, women have turned away from the ideal of the fulltime female caregiver and the male breadwinner model (Fraser 1997; Lewis 2001). Married/co-habiting women are no longer exclusively seen as care givers, but as combining paid work with care. The political scientist Joan Tronto labels this a 'gender revolution' (2013). It is indeed a change of enormous proportions, though not as abrupt as would be indicated by the term 'revolution'. This drive toward equality has been ongoing since the French Revolution, as the historian Joan Scott reminds us (Scott 1996). It has intensified during the last thirty years and has been aligned with various other forces (see also Fraser 2013 for a discussion of this). The gender revolution is still ongoing and changing gender identities for both women and men. For women it introduces the question of 'to care or not to care' and to resist a feminine code of moral obligations.

For men, the changes are less certain. Whether this push has abandoned what Tronto (1993) called 'privileged irresponsibility' is an open question. This concept refers to the privileges enjoyed by many men in relation to care toward others. Men have traditionally been seen as legitimately able to neglect or ignore other people's needs of care based on their privileged, gendered position. Connell argues that a transnational business masculinity has become hegemonic. This masculinity is characterized by egocentrism, conditional loyalties and a declining sense of responsibility to others (Connell 2005: 44). If this is true, a 'privileged irresponsibility' still exists as a hegemonic ideal and as an identity among a group of men.

In the five Nordic countries: Denmark, Finland, Iceland, Norway and Sweden, this push for de-gendering has been stronger than in the rest of the world, which most likely has been related to their 'passion for equality' (Hernes 1987). This does not mean that the gender system has become obsolete and replaced by a gender-neutral society. However, a new form of a caring masculinity has emerged (Holter 2003), especially in relation to fatherhood, where stress is placed on presence and attentiveness toward the family (Mosegaard 2006). Men's relationship to care has changed (Hjort and Nielsen 2003). One of the airline companies within Scandinavia, Scandinavian Airline Systems (SAS), ran a newspaper advertisement that aptly illustrates the changing image of fatherhood. The advertisement is about punctuality; the airline being on time enables the businessman not only to get to his meetings, but to get home in order to read a bedtime story for his child. A hegemonic picture of a caring father is now promoted among businessmen.

Changes are ongoing in the hegemonic forms of femininity and masculinity.[9] However, there is also a reproduction of established gender identities especially in relation to institutional elderly care. Here we witness a highly gender-segregated division of labor, with elderly care a predominantly female occupation and only modest changes in men's likelihood of working in elderly care. In Nordic countries today, men constitute about 10% of the care professionals or care workers in institutional elderly care (Andersson 2012; Hougaard, S., 2014, *Statistics Denmark*, personal communication). Despite political campaigns to actively recruit men, the number of men working in elderly care remains low (Hansen and Hjermov 2000; Andersson 2012). The push toward a de-gendering of care has been relatively weak in the elderly care sector, and there are still strongly gendered discourses toward the care workers (Warming 2012). Male care professionals are often met with different expectations by managers and recipients than their female colleagues. Despite the official discourse of gender equality, both managers and recipients of care reproduce gendered expectations; for example, elderly women attribute different characteristics to, respectively, women and men (Andersson 2012), and male care professionals may be viewed with suspicion concerning their sexual orientation—they are assumed to be gay (Warming 2012).

The de-gendering push has had different effects on the various forms of care. Care toward children, as we saw illustrated with the advertisement of the caring businessman, has changed, whereas institutional elderly care has experienced only modest changes in terms of more men becoming professional carers. Nor has the status of elderly care changed profoundly. This is surprising, if we consider the increasing illegitimacy of status differentials in the post-modern world (Fraser 2003). Changing gender identities does not necessarily lead to conflict unless these changes are perceived as controversial or threatening. On the other hand, the lack of changes in relation to gender equality for example, continuing low status, lower wages and misrecognition, may provide the spark for mobilization and struggles—as we have seen for example, in Denmark (Dahl 2009).

Globalizing and Migration

Globalization is a contested concept concerning its occurrence, content and impact (Giddens 1999; Walby 2009). By making it a noun, globalization becomes the object of de-politicization, as argued by Bourdieu (Bourdieu 2010: 200). Hence, in order to avoid a de-politicization I will use the concept as a verb, using Walby's definition of globalizing as a process of: 'increased density and frequency of international social interactions relative to local and national ones' (2009: 36). Globalizing processes are often thought to move us beyond time and place in processes of dis-embedding (Giddens 1991), achieving a kind of transcendence of space. However, most care needs are of the here and now; they cannot be postponed or moved to another space. Care, by its very nature, demands physical presence, constant attention, seeing to the needs of the person and his/her vulnerability and carrying out a variety of repetitive, mundane, and often distasteful tasks (Cooper 2007; Tronto 1993). In this sense, globalizing unsettles established care practices in various ways.

Globalizing is often seen as consisting of several elements of change, that is, economic, political, cultural and technological processes (Giddens 1999: 10). The globalizing process that is most relevant to care is the increasing migration in the world and its feminization, and how these processes relate to elderly care. In feminist sociology attention has been paid to the way globalizing increases the feminization of migrants (Koffman 2003). It is especially female migrants from poor countries who increasingly work in the Global North while leaving their children in the sending countries in the care of their families or paid carers. To describe this downside of globalizing, the American sociologist Arlie R. Hochschild has coined the concept of 'global care chains', which she defines as 'a series of personal links between people across the globe based on paid and unpaid work of caring' (2001: 131).

Whereas the 'global care chain' concept is originally based on research of women leaving their children behind and caring for other people's children, especially in the United States, the concept can be extended analytically to cover other parts of the world, to other groups such as elderly left behind and to female and male migrants caring for elderly in the Global

North. Whereas care-related migration is not new (Yeates 2009), it is a new phenomenon that a care squeeze in the West/Global North is now being eased by dependency on female migrants from poorer countries. Research on care chains indicates that they create suffering among the individuals/families left behind, and that they reduce social bonds in the communities from which female migrants have left. This situation creates new forms of care squeezes (Isaksen et al. 2008; Gheaus 2013). A 'care drain' takes place in the Global South.

However, there are also regional care chains. There is care migration within Europe, where we witness Eastern Europeans coming to the wealthier parts of Western Europe to work in the care sector (Lutz 2011; Isaksen 2010, 2011). And as Asian scholars have shown us, an increasing regional care migration takes place from less developed countries to higher income countries in Asia. Nurses and care workers from the Philippines and India increasingly migrate to Singapore to care for elderly people—both in their homes and in nursing institutions (Huang et al. 2012).

Globalizing processes and regional processes create new forms of care in transnational families. Hence, migrating (care) workers produce new kinds of families and sense of belonging (Lutz 2011). A new kind of transnational motherhood emerges (Avila and Hondagneu-Sotelo 1997; Parreñas 2001; Sørensen 2002), what some observers have labeled 'Skype mothering' (Lutz and Palenga-Möllenbeck 2009) involving Skype calls, text messages and e-mails. Perhaps we will also see the emergence of a 'Skype daughter-hood'/'Skype son-hood' (also covering in-laws) emerging, as daughters and sons leave their parents or parents-in-law behind in their migration.

Hitherto, we have seen the migration of carers. We are now also witnessing the migration of some—not so wealthy—elderly to nursing homes away from their country of origin. Around 2000 elderly Germans are now living in residential homes in Poland (*Frankfurter Allgemeine Zeitung*, 13 April, 2013) where costs are lower than in Germany. Not all elderly can afford residential/nursing homes in Germany and have therefore tried to look for affordable alternatives. This tendency is raising several issues, one of them being the increasing differentiation between elderly who can afford to stay in their country of origin and those who cannot. Another issue concerns the increasing concentration of the burden of care in particular regions of Europe, where some countries, such as Poland, are caring for 'their own elderly' as well as taking care of strangers who had not been previously been viewed as belonging to their community or nation.

Globalizing—and regional—processes are transforming care and easing care squeezes in wealthier countries and contexts. On the other hand, globalizing also creates more difficult conditions for care and care relations between family members or close others, producing new care squeezes in those communities that export care workers and care professionals. Care-related migration can also create instability, when work permits or visas expire for the foreign care worker leading to insecurity about future life plans. Conflicts between different notions of good care may arise as migrants with their own culturally or professionally embedded values of care encounter different cultural or institutional contexts. Migration within the EU creates a form of competition (so far unnoticed) between states as to who can provide the most affordable care, such as the competition between Poland and Germany for example.

Bureaucratizing

When care leaves the hands and minds of family and close others, it enters a different institutional context. This might be either the state or the market in both of which care has to fit into the institutional contexts and the dominant logic of a bureaucracy, thereby changing character. Bureaucracy is defined in its ideal typical terms by the German sociologist Max Weber as general rules (impartiality), division of labor (expertise) and hierarchy (control) (Weber 1976). Originally, this was a model that was scientifically deemed superior to previous organizational forms; only later did 'bureaucracy' become a term connoting inefficiency (Dahl 2015; Fine 2007; Gay 2013). Here I focus on bureaucratizing as the process of bringing care into the state, governing and transforming it and leaving out the market. When entering the sphere of state control, care enters a new institutional context shaped by bureaucracy and the existing logics of the state at a given time. Logics are forms of thinking and governing, and here we can speak of a 'bureaucratic logic'.

Logics, however, can also be more specific and concern the aim of care, or as I would say, the ideal of care (Dahl 2000; Hochschild 1995). Elderly care, for example, can be described in terms of a focus on care as compensation for what the elderly cannot do by themselves, such as when the certified home helper vacuums the floor. Alternatively, a different ideal of care could be described as 'rehabilitative', where 'the citizen is supposed to develop, regain or prevent a deterioration of his/her functions and abilities' by mobilizing their own personal resources (Kjellberg 2012; HMD translation). Applying the rehabilitative logic, the certified home helper motivates and trains the elderly person to vacuum the home by themselves, perhaps with some physical device that eliminates bending or lifting. These two different logics lead to different identities and practices of carers. At times these logics may clash, such that the interaction of these logics is an empirical question.

Bureaucratizing involves rules, which invariably entail a codification and standardizing of care routines. Codification is the process where care is brought into language, or a language to describe care is created. Standardization is here understood as a process that makes care uniform. Care practices are made comparable over time and space, the predictability of care is enhanced, and unwarranted variations are reduced (Björnsdottir 2013: 2). When care is codified, it enters discourse, that is, the existing horizons and vocabularies. As care has not (yet) had a voice of its own due to silencing, care must either fit into the existing vocabularies, or we must stretch the existing ones—or alternatively, invent new vocabularies. Struggles can arise in relation to bringing 'wordless care'—a concept coined by D. Stone (2000)—into language. Others use the concept of 'unnoticed' aspects of care (Ahrenkiel et al. 2013). Codification can raise issues concerning the proper way of articulating care. However, struggles can also arise concerning standards of care: Should there be standards? And if so, what kind of standards should there be? And what effects would such standards have on care practices? To what degree does the standardization or homogenization of services ignore the unique, individual needs of users, as has been observed in the Danish case

(Petersen and Schmidt 2003)? In sum, do standards and the observance of standards mean less time for hands-on care?

Bureaucratizing is different from neo-liberalism, a concept I will outline more thoroughly below. Bureaucratizing projects an ideal way of making decisions within the state, according to rational criteria and standards of justice and democracy. Bureaucracy is considered to ensure stability, continuity and consistency in the decisions and actions of bureaucrats (Gay 2013)—and of welfare professionals. Neo-liberalism presupposes a state—and a bureaucratic one too. Neo-liberalism, however, takes its point of departure in a critique of the state and its presumably inflated, controlling bureaucracy. With neo-liberalism, a particular image is created: that of a bureaucratic state burdened by red tape and inefficiency. At the same time, neo-liberalism promotes an ideology of being able to cure the sick state by reducing regulations and improving efficiency. In some countries, bureaucratizing and neo-liberalism have been distinctly different processes. In other countries, they have coincided, which perhaps has made it difficult to distinguish between them. And in still other countries, like the Nordic welfare states, the two processes have reinforced each other in the sense that an efficient, performance-oriented state also needs the kind of standards and regulations that characterize bureaucracy (Dahl and Rasmussen 2012). I shall now turn to neo-liberalizing.

Neo-liberalism and Neo-liberalizing

Neo-liberalism has been used in a broad, elusive manner (Larner 2000).[10] Basically, we can identify two distinct understandings of neo-liberalism. One understanding sees neo-liberalism as public policy and as organizational reforms within the state (Hood 1991; Christensen and Lægreid 2007). This understanding operates within the concept of NPM. Another understanding considers neo-liberalism from a perspective of ideology, discourse and governmentality (Dean 1999; Larner 2000). It is not concerned about particular reforms of the state, but more about the (political) shifts in our thinking, vocabularies and practices. My own understanding of neo-liberalism is inspired by Foucault and more specifically, by the American political theorist Wendy Brown, who defines neo-liberalism as a new political discourse that extends the logic of the market to all institutions and social action, that redefines the state as subservient to the economy, and produces calculating subjects instead of rule-abiding ones (Brown 2003). In short, neo-liberalism is about marketization, self-responsibilization, and increasing the role of the family and civil society.

I am trying to avoid totalizing neo-liberalism. Instead, we need to view it as a set of migratory logics inspired by the Canadian political scientist Aihwa Ong's view of neo-liberalism as a migratory set of practices (Ong 2007). Although neo-liberalism, in this particular theoretical understanding, includes phenomena that go beyond the state proper, I will limit my analytical focus to the state. Studying care through the lens provided by Dean, Brown and Foucault does not mean that I will ignore the insights of the literature on NPM and studies of specific reforms in specific, institutional contexts. These insights from studies of NPM are important for being able to identify the different ways in which a global discourse of neo-liberalism is translated into different contexts. Neo-liberalism is a new logic, suffusing our bodies and minds, thereby changing our ways of arguing and identifying ourselves and others. Moreover, neo-liberalism is a new form of governing, more subtle than governing through regulations and punishments. And it is ongoing as a social process, hence 'neo-liberalizing'.

With nearly three decades of neo-liberalism as a new form of regulation, research is increasingly considering whether neo-liberalism is entering a new phase and/or waning. Some scholars argue that NPM has become middle-aged and characterized by the increasing prevalence of paradoxes (Hood and Peters 2004), while others have gone so far as to pronounce NPM as 'deceased', arguing that we are beyond NPM and neo-liberalism (Dunleavy et al. 2006; Christensen 2012; Larner and Craig 2005). However, NPM is not dead; it lives on at various levels of regulation. We are in a new phase of NPM with the increasing prevalence of tensions, as I prefer to call it. Accompanying the choice and freedom that is so common to elderly care, we also have the production of more red tape. This is a direct result of increasing choice and contracting out in elderly care (Burau and Dahl 2013). The bureaucratizing of care has been reinforced by neo-liberalism in the Nordic countries, where state responsibility has been maintained, and the actual care labor outsourced to varying degrees (Meagher and Szebehely 2013). The competition between public and private providers of care brings with it a demand for codification, bringing the relatively 'wordless care' into the spoken. To ensure equal competition and that the mandated care is carried out, it has been argued that (more) codification is necessary. Codification in the Nordic countries has simultaneously been a process of creating more bureaucracy: more standardization, more rules, increasing division of tasks and more performance control. Regulations now describe the care routines to be performed, documenting and controlling the care work carried out by private as well as public providers. With a given amount of resources, this is simultaneously a process of reducing the practical aspects of doing care, replacing part of care with planning, describing and documenting care. NPM and neo-liberalism are themselves also changing, integrating ideas from outside the discourse into its existing horizon, that is, a co-optation is taking place (Clarke and Newman 1997). In the present context, the British political scientist Janet Newman and the Dutch sociologist Eveline Tonkens have argued that the dominant discourse of regulation in Europe has co-opted understandings and notions from earlier social movements, such as 'autonomy', and have been rewriting them into a new discourse of choice, responsibility and participation (Newman and Tonkens 2011).

Neo-liberalism has been, and still is, changing the conditions of care and thereby also the care provided. Changing conditions often mean that care professionals have to navigate in a new context, often having to rethink their identities. This new context can create tensions between the old and the new logics, thereby contributing to struggles about the content of care. Just as bureaucratizing is altering the way we think and act in relation to care, neo-liberalizing processes are also transforming care. However, we cannot consider neo-liberalism in a vacuum. Neo-liberalism is a dynamic discourse, changing over time and being translated into different institutional contexts, regime types and political constellations. By the term 'translation' here, I refer to the process of bringing a concept from one language into another that also takes account of the agency in translating traveling ideas (Newman and Tonkens 2011: 19). The Danish welfare state, as part of the cluster of social-democratic welfare states, has been hostile to certain aspects of neo-liberalism and NPM. They have been defined/as 'laggards' by Norwegian political scientists Tom Christensen and Per Lægreid (2007). Neo-liberalism has had to fit into existing logics, for example, the dominant logic of universalism that stresses equal access to services for citizens. In the Nordic countries, neo-liberalization changes care in three key ways: it tips the balance of power between the elderly and the professional care and their different forms of knowledge, it enforces a 'thin' notion of care[11] and finally, it enhances the ideology and practices of self-responsibilizing.

In a care context, the notion of 'choice' means a changing balance of power between the customer and the professional carer (Dahl et al. 2015b; Tonkens and Newman 2011). Increasing power is placed in the hands of the elderly, as the elder consumer occupies a position at the center of the decision-making process (Glendinning 2008). The elderly is seen as a knowledgeable, able and freely choosing individual in charge of his/her own life, able to make rational decisions about the quality and routine of their care in negotiations with the state, the caregiver authority or care firms. This changes the relationship with the professional carer, whose knowledge and autonomy is assigned lower priority compared to the power of the consumer, who is now in fact a customer choosing a 'service provider'. The changing terrain of the professional is played out in different national contexts and in different policy fields. Studies of the relationship between the professional and the user do not point to any one specific tendency. Tonkens and Newman (2011: 204–207) argue that although a change in the general terrain of the professional can be identified, the relationship between the professional and the user in a European context can be played out in three different ways, which they term the classical, negotiator and in a reflexive cooperation (ibid.). In some professions in certain countries, the classical relationship has survived despite transformative attempts. Here the professional is still the authority in relation to the client or patient. The second role, that of the negotiator, is identified in several European contexts. Here the citizens are viewed as experts in their own situation, which changes their relationship with carers and care-providing entities. Finally, reflexive cooperation occurs when, instead of negotiation, you have a shared project where the professional and the client/patient are bound together (Newman and Tonkens 2011: 2006–2007). Changing our gaze and considering neo-liberalism within a Nordic welfare regime, the autonomy of the professional carer is reduced by the standards that delimit their autonomy—and by the standardizing of the care service routine (Petersen and Schmidt 2003).

Neo-liberalism also brings a new notion of care: a 'thin' concept of care, which is aptly expressed by the notion of 'self-care'. It is a kind of hollowing out of care. From my feminist position, the concept of 'thin care' is a contradiction in terms: how can one care for oneself when caring means seeing and taking responsibility for helping someone else who is vulnerable? Neo-liberalism reframes the relationship between the state and the citizen. It rewrites and reduces the responsibilities of the state, thereby omitting aspects of care which were formerly part of the state-provided care regime. Some aspects of care have been silenced and have disappeared from the public eye. I shall later identify some of these elements, the way they have been silenced, and the way that there is a reduction of state responsibility in regard to the bodies and the space about which the state is supposed to care. Closely related to this hollowing out of care is the 'self-responsibilizing' processes at play in neo-liberalism. Neo-liberalism promotes a view of citizens as 'active', not as a possibility, but as an obligation (Dahl 2005).[12] Citizens are supposed to continually develop themselves even as elderly pensioners. The elderly become part of an activating regime that makes subjects turn toward themselves and reflect on what they can do to 'keep up' or 'improve their skills'—the latest example being the obligation of all Danish citizens to communicate with the state by e-mail, unless they can obtain a dispensation. Political issues are turned into ethical ones: they are individualized. This is a tension in neo-liberalism. On the one hand, the state extends its regulation by increasing its disciplining character, and on the other hand, it redraws the boundaries between our joint responsibility—embodied in the state—and the individual.

Transformations of such magnitude sometimes stir political debate at a national level. However, the national political elites are often part of the same transnational hegemonic discourse stressing choice, autonomy and cost-containment, discourses that circulate within the entire OECD (Marcussen 2002). Struggles are therefore more likely to take place at a local level: in the municipality or in the private homes of a citizen confronted with a care professional working under a new regime of performance criteria. Struggles are taking place with representatives of the state, with the providers—care professionals in firms and working freelance—and between them and the elderly 'user' or 'customer'. These struggles are about identities, extent and form of care. They are about who should do what, how they should do it, and for whom.

Neo-liberalism has redefined the state in the Nordic countries, although perhaps not as radically as in other European countries. It has been a dynamic discourse, adapting itself to the context of universalism and continuously co-opting new elements, such as 'quality' (Dahl 2012b) and 'the active citizen'. Although successfully rephrasing or even reinventing itself, neo-liberalism increasingly suffers from tensions. One example is between the stress on choice and the standardizing processes. Another tension is between the increasing regulation of elderly care and the narrowing down of the responsibility of the state for the welfare of the elderly. Reinventing the state as a service provider for 'customers' has had implications for the way professionals and users understand themselves. Their relationship—as service provider and customer—has also been reinvented and played out in three different versions—classical, negotiator and reflexive cooperation—changing the terrain of care in different ways. Needless to say, neo-liberalism is at odds with some of the existing logics of the Nordic welfare states, thereby creating the potential for struggles at different levels of the state concerning care.

A Changing Landscape of Elderly Care: Uncertainty, Complexity and Tensions

In this chapter, I have tried to understand the processes of transformation in elderly care in a Nordic context. There is no easy, unilineal narrative of progress or of decay. I would not diagnose the situation as a 'care crisis', but instead I would view it as a 'care squeeze'. The notion of 'care squeeze' itself is still a simplification of a more nuanced story of the seven complex interacting social and political processes that were described above: commodifying, professionalizing, late modernizing, de-gendering, globalizing, bureaucratizing and neo-liberalizing.

I prefer to avoid the straitjacket of judging the changing conditions of care as either an unequivocal improvement—the enlightenment story— or as a complete deterioration, as so many concerned feminists see it. Instead, we should view 'the care story' from a Foucauldian perspective, as one of changing conditions of care that create uncertainty, tensions, resistance and potential struggles. Care is currently one of the key fields of contestation where we are redefining ourselves, our social responsibilities and our communities. It is a contestation about who should do what—and how—for whom.

These processes involve agency and translation and are not inevitable. Each of the seven processes can generate changes that provide a space for struggles about identities and ideals of care. Now it is difficult—if not impossible—to summarize the complexity of the seven social and political processes and their intersection as well as their implications for the map of elderly care. So no final map will be outlined here. The seven processes are ongoing and difficult to distinguish empirically and analytically. Using a broad brush, I will instead give two examples that illustrate the difficulty in drawing a new map. The first example will show social and political processes reinforcing and at odds with each other—bureaucratizing and commodifying—and secondly, I will give an example of processes at odds with each other—bureaucratizing and late modernity.

Bureaucratizing and commodifying are examples of social and political processes that on one hand reinforce each other. Bureaucratizing is a process stressing general rules and emotional detachment in order to achieve fairness in the care given to the elderly. Commodifying turns care into a service to be bought and sold to a 'customer', with care entering the sphere of 'value for money'. In both processes, the elderly and the care professionals interact as strangers to each other; they are only buyers and sellers or customers and service providers.[13]

Some processes are internally ambiguous as well as at odds with each other and create space for tensions in the positions available. This is the situation for commodifying and late modernity. Late modernity is ambiguous in decreasing the possibilities for emotional attachment while increasing the need for emotional proximity. Commodifying is also ambiguous as it also decreases possibilities for emotional attachment as care becomes a commodity and simultaneously is demanding more emotional labor from the workers. The result of these contradictory processes is a tension-filled situation.

Notes

1. One could argue that there also exist more specific processes in elderly care. In so far as they exist, I have ignored them in my analysis in order to get a more general picture of the landscape.
2. Here intimacy is understood as the body work and emotional work involved in the private sphere not involving sexual relations.
3. The notion of 'stranger' is explained in depth in Chap. 3.
4. In my understanding of an emotional regime, I am inspired by Sara Ahmed and Nira Yuval-Davis (see Chap. 3 for an elaboration). Here it is suffice to say that that the regime delimits the legitimate and illegitimate forms of emotions. And emotional regimes differ, e.g. the emotional regime of a colder, neutral academia versus the emotional engagement of elderly care.
5. Re- and de-professionalizing will be discussed in more detail in Chap. 5 on state regulation and neo-liberalizing. In this section, I will therefore not discuss this issue.
6. The state can also be at a more regional level like the EU. Recently, we have witnessed that the EU has been engineering the foundations of professions through its financing of a small scale project, the 'European Care Certificate' (ECC). Please see Chap. 5 for an elaboration of this.
7. By complementing care the professional carer focuses upon care as a compensation for what the elderly cannot do by themselves e.g. when they vacuum the floor.
8. Issues related to gender and de-gendering will be taken up separately in the next section of this chapter.
9. Hegemonic masculinity is introduced by R.W. Connell (1987) and defined as 'always constructed in relation to various subordinated masculinities as well as in relation to women' (Connell 1987: 183). It has later been revised and specified by him together with another sociologist (Connell and Messerschmidt 2005).
10. I will return to the issue and concept of neo-liberalism in Chap. 5. Here I will also return to the more ambiguous aspects of neo-liberalism.

11. By a 'thin' notion of care I refer to a hollowed out form of care where elements are left out and not provided. So 'thin' is here a synonym for a 'skinny' form of care. I introduced this concept in an earlier article of mine (Dahl 2012a).

12. As I noted earlier in my discussion of late modernity, a new image of old age is simultaneously being promoted: that of healthy, active and successful aging.

13. On the other hand bureaucratizing and commodifying are at odds with each other. There is in commodifying an increasing focus upon the emotional performance thereby stressing different identities for the care worker and the care professional than in bureaucratizing where the ideal of affective neutraility prevails.

References

Ahmed, S. (2004). Affective economies. *Social Text, 22*(2), 117–139.

Ahrenkiel, A., et al. (2013). Unnoticed professional competence in day care work. *Nordic Journal of Working Life Studies, 3*(2), 79–95.

Andersson, K. (2012). Paradoxes of gender in elderly care: The case of men as care workers in Sweden. *NORA, 20*(3), 166–181.

Avila, E., & Hondagneu-Sotelo, P. (1997). I'm here, but I'm there: The meanings of Latina transnational motherhood. *Gender & Society, 11*(5), 548–571.

Björnsdottir, K. (2013). The place of standardization in home care practice: An ethnographic field study. *Journal of Clinical Nursing, 23*(9–10), 1411–1420.

Bourdieu, P. (2010). *Sociology is a martial art: Political writings by Pierre Bourdieu.* G. Shapiro (Ed.). New York: The New Press.

Brown, W. (2003). Neo-liberalism and the end of liberal democracy. *Theory and Event, 7*(1). https://muse.jhu.edu/article/48659. Accessed 27 July 2016.

Burau, V., & Dahl, H. M. (2013). Trajectories of change in Danish long term care policies—Reproduction by adaptation through top-down and bottom-up reforms. In C. Ranci & E. Pavolini (Eds.), *Reforms in long term care policies—Investigation institutional change and social impacts* (pp. 79–96). New York: Springer.

Christensen, T. (2012). Post-NPM and changing public governance. *Meiji Journal of Political Science and Economics, 1*(2), 1–11.

Christensen, T., & Lægreid, P. (2007). Theoretical approach and research questions. In T. Christensen & P. Lægreid (Eds.), *Transcending new public management: The transformation of public sector reforms* (pp. 1–16). Aldershot: Ashgate.

Clarke, J., & Newman, J. (1997). *The managerial state*. London: SAGE.

Connell, R. W. (1987). *Gender and power*. Cambridge: Polity.

Connell, R. W. (2005). Masculinities and globalization. In M. C. Zinn, P. Hondagneu-Sotelo, & M. A. Messner (Eds.), *Gender through the prism of difference* (pp. 36–48). Oxford: Oxford University Press.

Connell, R. W. (2011). *Confronting equality: Gender, knowledge and global change*. Cambridge: Polity.

Connell, R. W., & Messerschmidt, J. (2005). Hegemonic masculinities—Rethinking the concept. *Gender & Society, 19*(6), 829–859.

Cooper, D. (2007). 'Well, you go there to get off': Visiting feminist care ethics through a women's bath house. *Feminist Theory, 8*(3), 243–262.

Dahl, H. M. (2000). *Fra kitler til eget tøj – Diskurser om professionalisme, omsorg og køn*. Århus: Politica.

Dahl, H. M. (2005). A changing ideal of care in Denmark: A different form of retrenchment? In H. M. Dahl & T. R. Eriksen (Eds.), *Dilemmas of care in the Nordic welfare state: Continuity and change* (pp. 47–61). Aldershot: Ashgate.

Dahl, H. M. (2009). New public management, care and struggles about recognition. *Critical Social Policy, 29*(4), 634–654.

Dahl, H. M. (2012a). Neo-liberalism meets the Nordic welfare state—Gaps and silences. *NORA, 20*(4), 283–288.

Dahl, H. M. (2012b). Who can be against quality? A new story about home-based care: NPM and governmentality. In C. Ceci, K. Björnsdottir, & M. E. Purkis (Eds.), *Perspectives on care at home for older people* (pp. 139–157). Sted: Forlag.

Dahl, H. M. (2015). Regulering og velfærdsprofessionelle identitet(er). In B. Greve (Ed.), *Grundbog i socialvidenskab—5 perspektiver* (pp. 109–125). Frederiksberg: Nyt fra Samfundsvidenskaberne.

Dahl, H. M., & Rasmussen, B. (2012). Paradoxes in elderly care: The Nordic model. In A. Kamp & H. Hvid (Eds.), *Elderly care in transition—Management, meaning and identity at work* (pp. 29–49). Copenhagen: Copenhagen Business School Press.

Dahl, H. M., Hansen, A. E., Hansen, C. S., & Kristensen, J. E. (2015a). *Kamp og status—De lange linjer i et samtidsdiagnostisk og historisk-genealogisk perspektiv med særligt fokus på forholdet mellem pædagogiske institutioner, professioner og staten*. Copenhagen: U Press.

Dahl, H. M., Eskelinen, L., & Hansen, E. B. (2015b). Co-existing principles and logics of elder care: Help to self-help and consumer-oriented service. *International Journal of Social Welfare, 24*(3), 287–295.

Dahlager, L. (2001). I forebyggelsens magt. *Distinktion, 2*(3), 91–102.

Dahlerup, D. (1986). *The new women's movement. Feminism and political power in the USA and Europe.* London: SAGE.

Dean, M. (1999). *Governmentality—Power and rule in modern society.* London: SAGE.

Dunleavy, P., et al. (2006). New public management is dead—Long live digital-era governance. *Journal of Public Administration, Research and Theory, 16*(3), 467–494.

Eriksen, T. R. (2008). Fra kropslige erfaringer til forhandlingserfaringer—ændringer i den sygeplejestuderendes omsorgserfaringer fra 1987 til 2002. *Kvinder, Køn & Forskning, 17*(3), 33–42.

Eveline, J., & Bacchi, C. (2005). What are we mainstreaming when we are mainstreaming? *International Feminist Journal of Politics, 7*(4), 496–512.

Finch, J. (1989). *Family obligations and social change.* Cambridge: Polity.

Fine, M. D. (2007). *A caring society? Care and the dilemmas of human service in the twenty-first century.* Basingstoke: Palgrave Macmillan.

Foucault, M. (1991). Governmentality. In G. Burchell, C. Gordon, & P. Miller (Eds.), *The Foucault effect—Studies in governmentality* (pp. 87–104). Chicago: The University of Chicago Press.

Frankfurter Allgemeine Zeitung (2013, April 13).

Fraser, N. (1997). *Justice interruptus.* New York: Routledge.

Fraser, N. (2003). Social justice in the age of identity politics. In N. Fraser & A. Honneth (Eds.), *Redistribution or recognition? A political-philosophical exchange* (pp. 7–109). London: Verso.

Fraser, N. (2011, March 9). *The wages of care: Reproductive labor as a fictitious commodity.* Lecture at University of Cambridge. http://www.crassh.cam.ac.uk/gallery/video/nancy-fraser-the-wages-of-care-reproductive-labour-as-fictitious-commodity. Accessed 27 July 2016.

Fraser, N. (2013). Feminism, capitalism and the cunning of history. In N. Fraser (Ed.), *Fortunes of feminism—From state-managed capitalism to neo-liberal crisis* (pp. 209–226). New York: Verso.

Freidson, E. (2001). *Professionalism: The third logic.* Cambridge: Polity.

Gavanas, A. (2013). Elderly care puzzles in Stockholm. *Nordic Journal of Migration Research, 3*(2), 63–71.

Gay, P. (2013). New spirits of public management ... 'post-bureaucracy'. In P. Gay & G. Morgan (Eds.), *New spirits of capitalism? Crises, justifications and dynamics* (pp. 274–293). Oxford: Oxford University Press.

Gheaus, A. (2013). Care drain: Who should provide for the children left behind? *Critical Review of International Social and Political Philosophy, 16*(1), 1–23.

Giddens, A. (1991). *Modernity and self-identity—Self and society in the late modern age.* Stanford: Stanford University Press.

Giddens, A. (1992). *The transformation of intimacy—Sexuality, love and eroticism in modern societies.* Cambridge: Polity.

Giddens, A. (1999). *Runaway world.* London: Profile Books.

Glendinning, C. (2008). Increasing choice and control for older and disabled people: A critical review of new developments in England. *Social Policy and Administration, 42*(5), 451–469.

Hänsel, D. (1992). Wer ist der professionelle? *Zeitschrift für Pädagogik, 38*(6), 873–893.

Hansen, T. L., & Hjermov, B. (2000). *Integration af mænd og andre minoriteter på social- og sundhedsområdet.* Copenhagen: Teknologisk Institut.

Hardt, M. (1999). Affective labor. *Boundary 2, 26*(2), 89–100.

Hemmings, C. (2011). *Why stories matter—The political grammar of feminist theory.* London: Duke University Press.

Hernes, H. (1987). *Welfare state and woman power: Essays in state feminism.* Oslo: Universitetsforlaget.

Hjort, K., & Nielsen, S. B. (2003). Omsorg, maskulinitet og forskning i forandring—en indledning. In K. Hjort & S. B. Nielsen (Eds.), *Mænd og omsorg* (pp. 11–26). Copenhagen: Hans Reitzels forlag.

Hochschild, A. R. (1983). *The managed heart: The commercialization of human feeling.* Berkeley: The University of California Press.

Hochschild, A. R. (1995). The politics of culture: Tradition, cold modern, post modern and warm modern ideals of care. *Social Politics, 2*(3), 331–346.

Hochschild, A. R. (2001). Global care chains and emotional surplus value. In W. Hutton & A. Giddens (Eds.), *On the edge – Living with global capitalism* (pp. 130–146). London: Vintage.

Holter, Ø. G. (2003). *Can men do it? Men and gender equality—The Nordic experience.* Copenhagen: TemaNord.

Hood, C. (1991). A public management for all seasons. *Public Administration, 69*(1), 3–19.

Hood, C., & Peters, G. (2004). The middle aging of new public management: Into the age of paradox? *Journal of Public Administration, Research and Theory, 14*(3), 267–282.

Huang, S., Yeoh, B. S. A., & Toyota, M. (2012). Caring for the elderly: The embodied labour of migrant care workers in Singapore. *Global Networks, 12*(2), 195–215.

Isaksen, L. W. (2010). Transnational care—The social dimension of international nurse recruitment. In L. W. Isaksen (Ed.), *Global care work—Gender and migration in the Nordic countries* (pp. 137–157). Lund: Nordic Academic Press.

Isaksen, L. W. (2011). Gendering the stranger: Nomadic care workers in Europe—a Polish-Italian example. In H. M. Dahl, M. Keränen, & A. Kovalainen (Eds.), *Europeanization, care and gender global complexities* (pp. 141–151). London: Palgrave Macmillan.

Isaksen, L. W., Devi, S. U., & Hochschild, A. R. (2008). Global care crisis: A problem of capital, care chain, or commons? *American Behavioral Scientist, 52*(3), 405–425.

Jensen, K., & Tveit, B. (2005). Youth culture—A source of energy and renewal for the field of nursing in Norway. In H. M. Dahl & T. R. Eriksen (Eds.), *Dilemmas of care in the Nordic welfare state—Continuity and Change* (pp. 161–175). Aldershot: Ashgate.

Jessop, B. (2008). Karl Marx. In R. Stones (Ed.), *Key sociological thinkers* (pp. 49–62). Basingstoke: Palgrave Macmillan.

Johnson, T. (1995). Governmentality and the institutionalization of *expertise*. In T. Johnson (Ed.), *Health professions and the state in Europe* (pp. 7–24). London: Routledge.

Jones, I. R., & Higgs, P. F. (2010). The natural, the normal and the normative: Contested terrains in aging and old age. *Social Science and Medicine, 71*(8), 1513–1519.

Kjellberg, P. K. (2012). *Fra pleje og omsorg til hverdagsrehabilitering—Erfaringer fra Fredericia kommune.* Dansk Sygehus Institut: power points. http://www.uin.no/omuin/fakulteter/phs/konferanser/Documents/Erfaringer%20fra%20Fredericia.pdf. Accessed 19 Jan 2015.

Koffman, E. (2003, January 21–22). *Women migrants in the European Union.* Paper presented at the conference: The Economic and Social Aspects of Migration, Brussels.

Larner, W. (2000). Neo-liberalism: Policy, ideology and governmentality. *Studies in Political Economy, 63,* 5–25.

Larner, W., & Craig, D. (2005). After neoliberalism? Community activism and local partnerships in Aotearoa New Zealand. *Antipode, 37*(3), 401–424.

Larsen, L. T. (2013). Governmentalisering af velfærdsprofessionerne. *Dansk sociologi, 24*(3), 37–63.

Larsson, M. S. (1977). *The rise of professionalism.* Berkeley: University of California Press.

Lewis, J. (2001). The decline of the male breadwinner model. *Social Politics, 8*(2), 152–169.

Lutz, H. (2011). *The new maids—Transnational women and the care economy.* London: ZED Books.

Lutz, H., & Palenga-Möllenbeck, E. (2009, April 22–23). *The care chain concept under scrutiny—Female Ukrainian/Polish care migrants and their families left behind.* Paper presented at the conference Care and Migration, Frankfurt.

Marcussen, M. (2002). *OECD og idéspillet—Game over?* Copenhagen: Hans Reitzels Forlag (Magtudredningen).

Martinsen, K. (1994). *Fra Marx til Løgstrup: Om etik og sanselighed i sygeplejen.* Copenhagen: Munksgaard.

Meagher, G., & Szebehely, M. (Eds.). (2013). *Marketization in Nordic eldercare: A research report on legislation, oversight, extent and consequences.* Stockholm: Department of social work.

Mosegaard, M. (2006). Nærvær giver fædre autoritet. *Webmagasinet FORUM.* Downloaded at: http://kvinfo.dk/webmagasinet/naervaer-giver-faedre-autoritet. Last accessed 27 July 2016.

Newman, J., & Tonkens, E. (2011). Introduction. In J. Newman & E. Tonkens (Eds.), *Participation, responsibility and choice—Summoning the active citizen in Western European welfare states* (pp. 9–28). Amsterdam: Amsterdam University Press.

O'Rourke, H. M., & Ceci, C. (2013). Re-examining the boundaries of the 'normal' in ageing. *Nursing Inquiry, 20*(1), 51–59.

Ong, A. (2007). Neoliberalism as a mobile technology. *Transactions of the Institute of British Geographers, 32*(1), 3–8.

Parreñas, R. (2001). Mothering from a distance: Emotions, gender, and intergenerational relations in Filipino transnational families. *Feminist Studies, 27*(2), 361–390.

Parsons, T. (1964). *Essays in sociological theory.* New York: The Free Press.

Petersen, L., & Schmidt, M. (2003). *Projekt fælles sprog.* Copenhagen: Akademisk Forlag.

Pickard, S. (2010). The 'good carer': Moral practices in late modernity. *Sociology, 44*(3), 471–487.

Saraceno, C. (1997). *Family, market and community, Social policy studies no. 21.* Paris: OECD.

Scott, J. (1996). *Only paradoxes to offer.* Cambridge: Harvard University Press.

Sørensen, N. N. (2002). Transnationaliseringen af husmoderlige pligter. *Kvinder, Køn & Forskning, 11*(2), 9–19.

Squires, J. (2007). *The new politics of gender equality.* Basingstoke: Palgrave Macmillan.

Stone, D. (2000). Caring by the book. In M. H. Meyer (Ed.), *Care work, gender, labour and the welfare state* (pp. 89–111). London: Routledge.

Tonkens, E., & Newman, J. (2011). Active citizen, activist professionals— The citizenship of new professionals. In J. Newman & E. Tonkens (Eds.), *Participation, responsibility and choice—Summoning the active citizen in Western European welfare states* (pp. 201–215). Amsterdam: Amsterdam University Press.

Tronto, J. (1993). *Moral boundaries*. New York: Routledge.

Tronto, J. (2013). *Caring democracy: Markets, equality and justice*. New York: New York University Press.

Ungerson, C. (1997). Social politics and commodification of care. *Social Politics, 4*(3), 362–381.

Walby, S. (2009). *Globalization & inequalities: Complexity and contested modernities*. London: SAGE.

Warming, K. (2012). *Mænd i omsorgsfag, Ph.D. thesis*. Roskilde: Department of Society and Globalisation, Roskilde University Press.

Weber, M. (1976 [1921]). *Wirtschaft und gesellschaft*. Tübingen: J.C.B. Mohr.

Witz, A. (1992). *Professions and patriarchy*. London: Routledge. www.eccertificate.eu. Last accessed 27 July 2016.

Yeates, N. (2009). *Globalizing care economies and migrant workers—Explorations in global care chains*. London: Palgrave Macmillan.

3

Theorizing Elderly Care

In theorizations of care, the question traditionally posed is: *What is care?* Researchers such as Tronto (1993), Bubeck (1995) and Barnes (2012) have posed the question in this way, to name but a few within this vast theoretical field. They have outlined analytical dimensions of care (Tronto 1993, 2013), a circle of care (Bubeck 1995), and differentiating between relations, values and practices in care (Barnes 2012). To frame the question in this way risks essentializing care and neglecting the different forms of care which take place in different fields and different contexts. It also risks neglecting the changing conditions of care, and—as I have shown in the previous chapter—how these sociopolitical processes have radically changed care. We observe the increasing fragmentation of care and tensions between the various ongoing processes such as commodifying and late modernity, which promote both detachment and closeness at the same time.

I believe that '*What is care?*' is the wrong question to pose; therefore, I want to turn the question upside down, for it is more relevant to consider the requirements for theorizing care if we want to take into account the changing conditions of care and our ability to understand the kinds of struggles that occur in the care landscape. In order to identify struggles, we need to be more attentive to power. Several care researchers

© The Author(s) 2017
H.M. Dahl, *Struggles In (Elderly) Care*,
DOI 10.1057/978-1-137-57761-0_3

have argued that we need to focus on the potential connections between care and power and that we need a more complex theorization of power (Beasley and Bacchi 2007; Hankivsky 2014). It is often the case that if power is referred to at all in care studies, it is theorized as dominance; for example, the British social scientists Hockey and James (1993) focus on the Western domination discourse in its infantilizing of aging. Care as dominance is an important aspect of its theorizing, but we also need to pay attention to resistance to dominant understandings or ways of doing care, and to struggles about different ideals of care as well as the ways care can empower people. My attempt to introduce power more systematically and more broadly in care studies is based on a Foucauldian notion of power, stressing its dual aspects of productivity and repressiveness as well as—individual and collective—resistance and struggles as daily occurrences. So my question becomes: *How are the changing conditions of care and an attention to power and struggles reframing our theorizing about care?* Thus, the key question turns from a 'What is…' to a 'How are…' question, directing our gaze to more contemporary conditions of care and the increasing prevalence of struggles about care in various ways and various sites.

Building on the changing conditions of care and a theorization of power, I argue that we need to rethink care as an assemblage of care involving strangers, who are undergoing struggles between the different logics framing care and as part of affective regimes. Instead of thinking of care as embedded in relationships of care and in an ethics of care, it is more fruitful to think of care as an assemblage characterized by contingency and fragmentation of the care provided. And instead of thinking of care as provided by kin/close others in domestic settings, let us expand the notion of care as being provided only partly by kin/close others, but also by strangers, be it care workers, professionals and/or volunteers. And instead of thinking in dilemmas of care—and of ethics—we need to think in terms of logics that can be identified empirically—that are potentially changeable—and how they struggle to obtain the upper hand in the way care—and good care—is understood. Finally, care is often thought of as being good if combined with empathy and compassion. However, care is neither just about individual emotions, nor about exclusively positive, pleasant ones. Care is part of emotional regimes of togetherness, joy, gratitude, suffering and embarrassment, just to mention a few affects. Here I integrate concepts from different academic fields and traditions into a framework that will enable us to see neglected struggles.

To theorize care is not an uncontroversial question, and it includes an epistemological aspect. Lately, it has been argued that it is difficult to say anything in general about care, as we seem to be overwhelmed by the varieties of care in particular sites and national contexts. This chapter argues for the necessity of rigorous theorizing of care, not in order to define care in an overarching and general way, but rather to describe care from a specific, feminist position, to map out the struggles which define and structure the landscape of elderly care. In this sense, I try to describe the current situation from my particular position, embedded in contemporary discourses and situations of care. I do not speak from a privileged position outside the Archimedean circle. I will now describe the existing theory—or to be more specific, the dominant approach within existing theory—from my own feminist perspective and point out some of its shortcomings in order to lay the groundwork for an alternative view of care that foregrounds the struggles in a care landscape.

Existing, Dominant Theory, and Bringing Power Back In

The question '*What is care?*' has been considered directly and indirectly in feminist theorization of care (Tronto 1993; Bubeck 1995; Barnes 2012; Martinsen 1994; Noddings 1984; Graham 1991; Wærness 1980, 1987), just to mention a few of the scholars in this expanding research field. This theorization has thus made us recognize care as a specific social phenomenon that the founding fathers of social science had overlooked. Karl Marx introduced the notion of 'reproduction', but he only saw it as a precondition for 'production' (Widerberg 2007). Reproduction as such had no independent value, and his attention was geared to the political-economical rules behind the development of 'production'. Max Weber (1921) introduced four rationalities in order to understand motivations for action on a more general level, and he introduced the concept of 'affective rationality'. This was one rationality guiding social actions—and

ɔt to be equated with what we today label 'care work'. The
ist care theorists and the more recent ones have made us real-
ɪre is a social phenomenon, requiring analytical concepts to
various elements, its different forms, its changing conditions
and ɪts ɪmportance for humankind in a broad sense. In the process of
theorizing, a field of research has been established bringing together
research from different fields of care, in different national contexts and
from different positions. The field of research is loosely knit together,
and when labeling it a 'feminist' theorization of care, this should not
be taken to mean that it is a homogenous field with a single feminist
voice.[1] Below I will describe the most dominant voices within this field,
often referred to as 'the ethics of care', but I will also describe other, less
influential voices.

Ethics of care spans the largest and oldest field of care research and theorizing. In this way, it is the dominant—or most typical—way of thinking about care in research. It originated in a scientific dispute between
two psychologists about the character of ethical rules and child development (Gilligan 1982) and the importance of gender (Hankivsky 2014).
Soon the ethics of care evolved into a broader literature concerned with
the moral implications of care from the most local to the broader social
and political settings of care in the modern age, including both caring
attitudes and practices (Tronto 1993, 2013; Robinson 1999). In general,
this school has not paid attention to struggles and only scant attention
to power.

Since the publication of the American psychologist Carol Gilligan's *In
a Different Voice* (Gilligan 1982), the theorization of care has been linked
to morality and ethics. Since the beginning of Greek philosophy, ethics
has been the field of individual decision-making in situations of moral
conflict, often between different, universal values and rules. Gilligan's
book sought to frame care as an issue of ethics, and in doing so it broke
radically with the existing tradition of ethics. The American political scientist Susan Hekman described Gilligan's work as constituting an epistemological break concerning the understanding of morality and the
subject (Hekman 1995). The field of morality was expanded, and the
understanding of the subject was radically changed from an independent
person to a person in a web of relations with others. But this person

also had to choose between different moral principles for exar
was a dilemma between universal rules and more contextual
ones. Framing care in terms of ethics means that care becom
about individuals, obligations, rules and relationships although with the
insights of Gilligan in a specific context. In this way, it is also bound to a
normative dimension. Viewing care exclusively through the prism of ethics, however, risks overlooking how the conditions for providing care have
changed in various ways. It is these changing conditions that have altered
the context of decision-making from an exclusively ethical decision-making in care. Understanding care exclusively within a framework of an ethics of care means that these theorists cannot see power and struggles, as
the ethics of care approach is concerned with what ought to be the right
decision and action. In an ethics of care approach, conflicts are explained
as a clash between opposing values and rules, for example, whether to
steal expensive medicine to save a mother's life, or leave her to die. This is,
in fact, Heinz's dilemma between two options (Gilligan 1982).

The American political scientist Joan Tronto was the first scholar to
explicitly raise the issue of power in relation to care (1993). She theorized
care as involved in relations of power (1993) and showed how power
penetrates the care landscape (2010). In her book, she investigated care as
a system of unequally distributed care between gender, classes and races.
Differentials in power were therefore also a characteristic of the—gendered—system of care. In her view, conflicts arose between different care
professionals not because of a value conflict but because of contests about
the distribution of resources (1993). As mentioned in the last chapter
Tronto introduced the notion of 'privileged irresponsibility' referring to
some men who occupy a supposedly privileged class and gender position These men neglected the caring needs of others, but they were not
held responsible. In this sense, the ethics of care was gendered making
it legitimate for men—or at least some groups of men—to neglect others and their caring needs. In a later article investigating the elements of
good care, Tronto mentions paternalism as a misuse of power (2010) and
stresses the thoroughly political nature of care in institutional settings.
Tronto's project is to redirect our attention from exclusively focusing
upon ethics of care to politics and institutions with values and cultures
(Tronto 2010).

Here Tronto seems to be moving away from her ethics of care and justice perspectives. For Barnes, there are also doubts. For example Barnes also states that we need to 'address the question of the relevance and usefulness of an ethics of care in diverse contexts' (2012: 8), that is, we need to reflect upon how we think about care. In this way, the ethics of care literature seems less confident about the foundations of an ethics of care than it used to be. And several scholars have criticized the ethics of care for a neglect of the relationship between care and power (Beasley and Bacchi 2007: 284) and called for more 'nuanced and complex accounts of power' (Hankivsky 2014: 159).

Consequently, the Anglo-American theorization of care has suffered from a tendency to make care indirectly an issue of good or bad actions; for example, in situations of care neglect or inadequate care. Tronto and other feminists have stressed the importance of care and its unequal distribution, that is, the injustices of care concerning obligations, work and pay. However, I suggest to shift the analytical framework from ethics to thinking in terms of logics—ways of thinking—power and struggles between contesting logics. Before we can consider other, new ways of theorizing care, however, let us examine three other schools of care that are not as dominant as the ethics of care: reproductive labor (Hochschild 2001, 2003), social policy[2] and the double perspective.

Three Other Straitjackets of Our Thinking

The three schools reproductive labor, social policy and double perspective—i.e. carer-elderly relationship—while being less influential in the field of care studies, are nevertheless important. The distinction between these three schools draws on existing literature (Barnes 2012) and on my own, earlier research identifying contrasts between an Anglo-American and a Nordic tradition (Dahl 1997). Probably, this distinction does not do justice to the way specific researchers are drawing on and are inspired by other schools, as boundaries between schools are transgressed when researchers become inspired by other researchers and new ideas.[3] In my view, however, the three schools are still distinctive. Although each school has provided important insights on care, they neglect the way care can be the object of various kinds of struggles, and the way power is spun into the web of care. Let us begin with the first of the three schools, that of reproductive labor.

The reproductive labor approach focuses on the impact of globalizing processes on care from a gender perspective, based on an enhanced Marxist understanding of exploitation. This school studies how the care squeeze combined with globalizing processes has created new forms of care in global care chains as mentioned in the previous chapter (Hochschild 2001; Isaksen 2007; Isaksen et al. 2008; Parreñas 2001; Yeates 2009). Global care chains refer to a chain of care as socio-emotional labor given from one person to another. Female migrants from economically poor countries increasingly work in better-off countries, leaving their own children behind to be cared for by other relatives or paid carers. The separation of female migrants from their children produces suffering on both sides (Hochschild 2001, 2003), and migration erodes social solidarities in the sending communities (Isaksen et al. 2008). Care is basically seen as reproductive labor that is extracted from the—female—live-in migrant by a global capitalist system that solves its needs of care by turning it into a commodity. Exploitation and neo-colonial relations are produced (Sarvasy and Longo 2004; Tronto 2011). Within this school, struggles have not been at the center of attention. Little agency has been allotted to the migrating carers apart from analyzing their original decision to migrate (Spanger and Dahl 2010). Until very recently, this tradition did not focus on the role of the state (Williams 2011; Spanger et al. manuscript).

The second school is that of the social policy care literature, and it is often comparative in scope. Within the social policy literature, analytical attention is paid to the macro level of different care and welfare systems, their characteristics and changes. In the words of Barnes, social policy literature on care addresses the political economy of care, gender, individualism and collectivism in the assignment of responsibilities for care, changing policy orientations, and how they impact on specific care policies (Barnes 2012: 147). As argued by Barnes, little attention is paid to care as a value nor to specific practices of care (Barnes 2012: 175). This tradition seems to be in a process of change, as one of its main advocates has integrated ideas about recognition and developed theorizing to include different claims for mobilizing and resisting discourses from above (Williams 2010).

The third tradition is that of a double perspective of care, which investigates both the conditions of the caregiver/the professional carer and the recipient as well as the role of the state in welfare/policies on elderly care (Wærness 1987). The double perspective attends to both the caregiver and the recipient of care in terms of changing conditions and policies of elderly care for example (Andersson 2012).

These three schools reflect a strong sociological bias trying to understand the meanings, dynamics and effects of care and care work. Together, they have contributed important insights about ethics—or the lack of ethics—in political reasoning and in political theory, the interrelationship between welfare systems and the provision of care, the unintended effects of globalizing care and the necessity of researching care from a double perspective, including caring for the carer (as also stated by Kittay et al. 2005). However, the schools also suffer from intellectual straitjackets, neglecting issues of power, tensions, struggles and resistance about care and its regulation under the new conditions of care as well as the intensification of struggles.

Power-over and Power-to in Care

Care research has begun to acknowledge its insufficient attention given to power, and the need to theorize it in a more complex and nuanced way. In the previous two sections, I have shown that the four schools of theorizing care have intellectual blindfolds that prevent them from seeing issues of power. If they are aware of power, it is only as power within a given relationship, as power-over either on an individual basis or in a systemic way, for example, 'privileged irresponsibility'. It is certainly not new today to claim that power can be both repressive and productive, as Foucault did (Foucault 1980). Feminist and female philosophers have also stressed the various productive aspects of care, such as various understandings of empowerment (Emmet 1953–1954; Ferguson 1987; Hartsock 1985; Bubeck 1995). So how can we broaden our understanding of power?

Foucault does not present a theory of power. Instead, he presents an analytics of power, enabling us to study power and its vehicles in various historical epochs. This analytic stresses that power is like a coin with two sides, the repressive and the productive:

> What makes power hold good, what makes it accepted, is simply the fact that it doesn't only weigh on us as a force that says no, but that it traverses and produces things, it induces pleasure, forms knowledge, produces discourse. (Foucault 1980: 119)

Power produces new subjectivities and old ones. It is contingent, as no one holds power in his hands as a commodity—it is circulating, as in a netlike organization (Foucault 1980: 98). This makes power difficult to identify, more fluid than in traditional approaches to power. Resistance is not an exemption to power, but necessarily a part of power (Foucault 1978). In this netlike organization of power, there are many points of potential resistance. Power is exercised by everyone—and perhaps also everywhere— and 'ultimately nowhere' (Hartsock 1985: 170). A nurse is exercising self-surveillance in the way she enters the room of a dying elderly person, and a home helper is monitoring the actions of close others in relation to an elderly person suffering dementia. Power restrains one from doing something, as this would be inappropriate according to dominant discourses, and it is conducive to doing things in a particular way, as this is the right way to perform care in the given circumstances. In this sense, power is enabling for care recipients. Receiving care enables them to do something they otherwise could not have done, for example, going for a walk and having a proper meal served. Power-to could also have the form of having more energy, vitality such as stressed by Emmet (1953–1954). In the sphere of care, power-to could be seen as the increasing energy in an elderly person due to an emotional lift given by the care worker/professional carer performing care.

Power is also productive in a more collective way, as the German-American philosopher Hannah Arendt has argued:

> Power corresponds to the human ability not just to act, but to act in concert. Power is never the property of an individual; it belongs to a group and it remains in existence only so long as the group keeps together. (Arendt 1986: 64)

In this optic, a group of home helpers protesting in front of parliament has power to make claims about the need for change. Power is here a common capacity, but only for the period of this togetherness. The power vanishes the moment the group dissolves. Seeing power more broadly, as power-over and power-to, and as everywhere and potentially also as a collective ability, changes the way we think of care. Care becomes traversed by power, and resistance is potentially everywhere.

Using Foucault's Concept of Critique

From the early beginnings of the feminist theorization of care, the cultural, historical component of care has been recognized (Finch 1989; Tronto 1993; Wærness 1982). What is seen as care and the kind of needs identified and acted upon is seen as related to contemporary culture and context. For Tronto, this conventional element of care has been understood as a particular component in a universal phenomenon (1993). Care as a universally occurring phenomenon was seen as relatively easy to discern in reality, and feminist theory of care has exposed a relatively realistic epistemological position concerning what we can know about care—and how. However, recent theorizations and investigations of care have taken a different starting point than this relatively realist epistemology. Instead, they have studied concrete care practices and paid attention to different sites of care, forms of care and—national—contexts (Cooper 2007; Barnes 2012; Mol 2008). They have exchanged high level theorizing for a more focused attention to concrete practices of care and different institutional contexts, for example, work and communities. Cooper argues that instead of high level and normatively infected theorizing about care, we need to study concrete practices of care and discern the prevalent norms about care (2007). Annemarie Mol carries out ethnographic fieldwork in Dutch diabetes care clinics in order to identify and describe the practices at work. In her study of diabetes treatment, Mol identifies two different kinds of practices: a logic of choice and a logic of care.[4] She does not attempt to say anything about care beyond her particular study. However, she wants to contribute to the improvement of health care (Mol 2008: 89) by highlighting patients' everyday experiences of bad health care. For Mol, improvements of care can be achieved by listening and being more attentive to the specificities of every single patient. From these case studies, we can learn about the conditions for care in specific fields—and how potential negotiations and struggles are played out. However, Cooper and Mol both adopt a nominalist position, describing care practices and leaving normative issues of good or bad care to be defined contextually by the social agents involved in care relations in a particular space and time. Although I am sympathetic with this position, I will take a slightly different position, inspired by Foucault.

With the linguistic turn in science, Lyotard (1984), Foucault (1978), Wittgenstein (1989) and Haraway (1988) argued against grand meta-narratives. Instead, they saw our knowledge as more situated, as always seen from a particular perspective. Does this mean that we end up in a relativist position? I believe not. The American philosopher Nancy Fraser has argued, together with the historian Linda Gordon in an essay from 1990, that there is a middle ground between a realist and a nominalist position (Fraser 1997: 209). So I will not present grand meta-narratives of improving elderly care—the enlightenment story—or crisis of care—the eschatological one—nor will I exclusively accept what has often been termed the nominalist and relativist position of Foucault. Instead, I will make ontological claims about Westernized societies and states in the current era that have the character of large-scale empirically grounded narratives—which are not grand meta-narratives). I use the concept of critique introduced by Foucault in his interaction with one of Kant's important texts: *Was ist Aufklärung?* (Foucault 1997). Foucault sees critique as closely interwoven with the scientific field and with the work of a scientist. He argues that critique can help us relate reflectively to ongoing strategies by raising three kinds of questions. These are questions about, respectively, truth, ethics—legitimacy—and the rationale for introducing such strategies. Critique is about asking foundational questions such as: 'Is this an adequate description of what happens with care?'—truth. 'Are the political in-order-to reasons sound and ethically defensible?'—ethics. And finally, 'What are the reasons for applying different political strategies, for example, such as marketization and self-responsibilizing?' —rationale.

Whereas it is important to theorize care as grounded in specific care practices, it is also obvious that the societal processes outlined in Chap. 2, processes such as neo-liberalizing and globalizing work, are at work across different sites and forms of care. This is the way in which researchers can obtain the kind of knowledge about developments that the individual patient, client, sick child or elderly in need of care cannot have. And from this position, researchers can raise questions along the three dimensions of critique listed by Foucault. Researchers may know more than the recipients of care, although the recipients are important voices in care. As researchers, we can be more courageous, telling larger, sufficiently complex stories while being painfully aware that the stories we tell matter (Hemmings 2011). Hence, I believe that researchers can tell larger stories and simultaneously navigate between Scylla—the enlightenment narrative—and Charybdis—the eschatological narrative—while not falling into the trap of commitment to a single, meta-narrative.

Relatedness, Assemblage of Care and Strangers

To theorize '*What is care?*' seems, on the one hand, important for social science in order to delimit what it is we are studying. On the other hand, it seems like a fruitless discussion if this issue remains at a rather abstract, systemic level, or at an individual level of responsibilities and sensibilities that evade engagement with the changing conditions of care practice. The seven processes of change outlined in the previous chapter work as conditions of possibility for the way care can be conceptualized and provided at the contemporary scene. If there has been no scientific attention to the way these changes reframe identities and communities, we need to broaden our optic and change the key question we are considering. Instead of asking 'What is', we need to ask, '*How are the changing conditions of care and another understanding of power changing the way we see care?*'

The seven macro-processes outlined in the previous chapter change the landscape of care substantially by fragmenting care—splitting or slicing care up—creating uncertainty and contingency, and creating tensions through their ambiguous and at times contradictory nature. This is the case, for instance, when the commodification of care makes professional carers replaceable, and when care professionals turn more post-modern, concerned more with communication and self-realization instead of directing their energies toward the 'other'. This is also the case when post-modernizing creates a plurality of family forms and destabilizes the family, making relations more fragile and contingent. The contemporary processes of neo-liberalizing bring marketization, customers' choice and self-responsibilizing to the forefront, challenging the knowledge and the traditional role of the professional.

So how can we think about theorizing care when the conditions change, and care becomes more complex, fragmented and contingent? In many theorizations, care is often tied together with a dyadic understanding of care as involved in a relationship. This approach extends back to the founding mothers of the feminist theorization of care in the British context of elderly care as primarily informal and provided by family in the private home. Over two decades ago, Tronto criticized this dyadic understanding (Tronto 1993: 103) and introduced a notion of a 'web of care', indicating the lack of a clear beginning and end (Tronto 2010). Others have recently used the notion of a 'web of social relations' (Mahon and Robinson 2011). Instead of stable relationships/relations, I use the concept of 'relatedness', as it signifies instability, contingency and flexibility. Relatedness is more appropriate for a situation today, when more people take part of care for a specific person, involving some kind of division of labor between professional carers, care workers, family members and close others, some living close by, others far away.[5] 'Relatedness' fits the condition of care as being spatially and temporally fragmented by late-modernizing, globalizing, commodifying and professionalizing—to name a few.

When attempting to choose an analytical concept that was best suited to describing this relatedness and instability, I adopted the analytical concept of 'assemblage' introduced by the French philosophers Gilles Deleuze and Félix Guattari (Deleuze and Guattari 1988). With the 'assemblage' concept, Deleuze and Guattari strike a balance between the ephemeral and emergent on the one hand, and structure and order on the other (Marcus and Saka 2006). 'Assemblage' is a concept that tries to complement Foucault's desire for order in his application of discourse with a concept stressing disorder (Legg 2006). An assemblage is an unpredictable collection of connections. Or in other words, an assemblage is an intermingling of bodies in a society traversed with all kinds of emotions (Deleuze and Guattari 1988: 90). It has a contingent spatial existence as the processes of territorialization and de-territorialization are ongoing (Deleuze and Guattari 1988: 503–505).[6]

To use the concept of 'assemblage' enables us to see care as something unpredictable (not in relatively stable relationships) and not necessarily always taking place. Care is neither exclusively exercised in close relationships nor in care chains of interchangeable individuals. Instead, assemblages of close others, professional carers—migrant—carer workers and people happening to be passing by are those who actually carry out the care tasks. To rethink care as assemblage also means allowing for the failure of assemblages to provide—adequate—care at a given point in time. Failure here refers to neglect of care—the failure to see to care needs (Tronto 1993) or to 'the hiccups of inadequate care'—when state-financed or privately purchased care is insufficient or problematic (Hoppania and Vaittinen 2015).

The analytical concept of assemblage fits with the increasing fragmentation of care and the prevalence of 'strangers'. By strangers, I refer to new persons who are not previously known to the vulnerable person. Strangers could be of the same ethnicity or class as the vulnerable person, but they could just as well come from a different religious, ethnic and gendered background. The concept of a stranger is taken from Swedish sociologist Katarina Andersson, drawing on the writings of Julia Kristeva and Georg Simmel (Andersson 2007: 29–30).[7] Andersson understands the encounter with the stranger as potentially positive, but also as a threatening experience. The encounter may simultaneously create new possibilities and reproduce existing practices. In this sense, the meeting with a stranger creates both closeness and distance (Andersson 2007: 30). Unpredictability is part of this meeting; therefore the anxiety invariably associated with encountering any sort of stranger.

When the elderly person and her needs are attended to by a stranger, that is, a professional carer or care worker, then this might be the only time the person enters and leaves the assemblage. However, the stranger might return for further care visits, becoming a more intimate acquaintance for the elderly person, someone on whom they become emotionally dependent. Despite the creation of relative stability in the assemblage, positions are unstable. Professional carers and care workers come and go. Simultaneously, there are no stable and homogenous identities. One moment a care worker is providing care for the elderly person, and the next moment they exchange places, for example when the elderly is providing some emotional support to the care worker having recently lost her husband.

Contingency refers to the changing of places in a more literal sense too. Quoting a nurse theorist: 'everyone is vulnerable at different times in his or her life' (Rogers 1997). In this sense, there are no stable identities such as 'the professional carer' and 'the sick person'. The professional carer might suddenly become a vulnerable person in need of help. Thus, we are all vulnerable or, as already expressed in the Introduction, 'handicapped' or 'challenged' in one way or another. Seeing ourselves in this way as *always already vulnerable* also means distancing ourselves from a deficit model of care, where care is only about identifying the health and care problem and fixing it (Latimer 2012). Care is so much more than just fixing 'something'. Instead of a deficit model of care, Martha Fineman (2008) has introduced the concept of 'vulnerability', which refers to the 'universal, inevitable and enduring aspect of the human condition' (Fineman 2008: 8). A human being cannot avoid vulnerability—at some time in our lives we all become vulnerable, from when we are babies, sick from a virus, hit by a disaster or accident, or by the fragility of the aging body. Vulnerability brings the body—embodiment—into the picture, and discussions about materiality and the body have a long history in feminist theory. Fineman's insights about vulnerability have been subject to critique. Beasley and Bacchi (2007) have argued that her notion of vulnerability neglects the role of social institutions and of power. Their argument cannot be pursued here, but it certainly hints at some of the problems I have already identified about the under-theorization of care in the various schools of care studies.

Several scholars have argued that there is a problem about power in care ethics and research on care. However, none have provided the kind of rethinking of care that might enable an integration of power into care theory. In this section, I have argued that care cannot be seen as consisting of care relations, arguing instead for an approach based on care assemblages consisting of care workers, care professionals and close others in situations of relatedness with both strangers and known others.[8] By theorizing care in terms of assemblage, we can broaden our view of the involved persons, the kinds of conflicts and struggles occurring, and the assessment of continuity, quality and character of care.

Reframing Dilemmas into Struggles Between Different Logics

Difficult situations often occur in care, and there is an uncertainty among professional carers and care workers about how to cope with these situations. Theoretically, feminist theorists of care have so far identified these difficult situations as characterized by dilemmas (Stone 2000; Dahl 2000; Dahl and Rasmussen 2012). This, I believe, is related to the strong connection to the feminist ethics of care research. Deborah Stone introduces and lists some dilemmas of care: talk versus tasks, love versus detachment, specialness versus fairness, patience versus schedules, family relations versus work relations, and relationships versus rules (Stone 2000). In this way, Stone characterizes the different, and logically exclusionary ways—and principles—of providing (good) care. In my former work, I also identified three dilemmas: (1) care for oneself versus care for others, (2) love versus justice, and (3) love versus knowledge (Dahl 2000). Recently, a paradox between professionalization and standardization has been identified with the predominance of neo-liberalism in the Nordic welfare states (Dahl and Rasmussen 2012). Another way of describing this dilemma would be a dilemma between professional knowledge and bureaucratic rules. In addition, dilemmas concerning time have been identified and elaborated upon (Tufte and Dahl 2016).

Dilemmas point to tensions or clashes between different ways of seeing care when care moves out of the home and becomes market-based, a state responsibility, a civil society responsibility or a mixture of these. The dilemmas are depicted as a contradiction between different, logically excluding, principles and, in this way, as Catch-22 situations. Whatever you do, it is wrong. You can always be blamed for not acting according to one or another principle. However, by acknowledging their differences dilemmas could instead be reframed as struggles between competing ways of understanding good care. Hence, instead of identifying a dilemma between, say, 'talk versus tasks', the dilemma could be reframed as an example of a more general struggle about the ideal of care. Is good care more about talking and listening to the one needing some form of care, or is it more about getting some tasks done? Identifying struggles about the regulation of care are intensified and introduce new perspectives that were formerly defined as dilemmas seen as static and unavoidable. Sometimes paradoxes and dilemmas give rise to tensions and struggles.

Although the description of various dilemmas has directed our attention to clashing principles and practices of care, the 'dilemma' concept remains problematic. Dilemmas have 'misframed' the issue at stake as one of individual decision-making between two mutually exclusive principles of equal social value. The concept of 'misframing' is introduced by Nancy Fraser (Fraser 2008) and refers to the way the particular framing of a political question excludes an important dimension. The misframing occurs as the notion of 'dilemmas' tends to overlook the aspect of power in situations of care—and the agency of the participants in the network. Let me explain this further. As Stone mentions, there is a clash between love and detachment, that is, between the emotional involvement of family and the typically detached professional with his/her technical knowledge. Instead of seeing this as a dilemma, I suggest that we see it as a struggle between different logics and between ideals of good care. At different times, the logics of empathy/sympathy overrule the logic of technical knowledge about a specific sickness; on other occasions, technical expertise 'trumps' the engagement of loved ones, depending on the existing discourses about good care.

The ethics of care has provided important insights about care. It has also misframed some issues as being a question of dilemmas instead of seeing these issues as indications of ongoing struggles between competing and empirically identifiable and shifting logics.

Emotional Regimes

Some researchers have viewed care in terms of emotional involvement. The British social policy analyst Marion Barnes, for example, argues that 'ethical sensibilities [are] necessary to practice care' (Barnes 2012: 8). For Barnes, care involves a caring attitude, an attention toward others and their states of being. Feminist theorists of care have seen emotions and love as an integral part of care (Thomas 1993; Leira 1994) and often their focus is on the individual level. By focusing on the individual level and on the necessity of a specific—and positive—sensibility, the social embeddedness of the emotion is neglected. Likewise, the stress on exclusively positive emotions of attachment and caring leads to a neglect of negative emotions that invariably arise in the care context, feelings of estrangement, fatigue, resentment, being unappreciated, feelings of disgust and loneliness. As any caregiver knows, these emotions are often present in the care context, even when the vulnerable person is a close family member.

If we focus solely on the individual level, we risk neglecting how emotions expressed at the individual level are part of a larger system of socialized emotions, a socio-psychological field where proper and recognizable emotional behavior is learned. This is not to say that we are social dopes; rather, it is because the individual does not exist on an island, to paraphrase Ludwig Wittgenstein. I would like to use the concept of a 'regime' to capture the specific way in which emotions circulate at an abstract level. A regime is a field delimiting how we can behave in a given institutional context, that is, be recognized as legitimate caring subjects. The concept of emotional regimes is taken from British sociologist Nira Yuval-Davis (2011), and the concept of legitimate and recognizable subjects is used by American philosopher Judith Butler (Butler 1990). Academia, for example is an emotional regime whose emphasis on emotional detachment stands in stark contrast to the emotional regime of care work; each regime specifies different legitimate subjects. A regime is a site of what can be said and done, and thereby delimiting who you are—and can be—as an academic in one case, and for our purposes here, as a care worker, family member, close others and professional carer. A regime in this sense prohibits what can be felt and done, marking boundaries of proper behavior, also prescribing proper behavior, and is simultaneously open to change by reinterpretations and resistance. A regime is neither a closed nor a static concept.[9]

In line with the British feminist sociologist Sara Ahmed, I see care as part of several circulating emotional regimes (2004). Emotions are seen to circulate between bodies and between objects—and inscribed on surfaces of bodies. Emotions are relational and involve relations of 'towardness' or 'awayness' (Ahmed 2004: 8). In this sense, we cannot take certain emotions in care for granted. We have to see them as part of emotional regimes. Care, therefore, is not to be equated with an emotional regime. However, all care work is performed within an emotional regime—and a knowledge regime.[10] Emotional regimes differ even within care. There is an emotional regime for caring for close others and an emotional regime for caring for strangers when employed by the state care agency or care company. In this sense, emotions are not something immanent in persons. They are managed and governed at various levels. That care is managed is not new. The American sociologist Arlie R. Hochschild introduced the notion of emotional labor in her groundbreaking study of the work of airline stewardesses (Hochschild 1983). Hochschild identified how stewardesses worked with their own emotions to create a particular atmosphere in the cabin and to suppress feelings of anger in relation to difficult passengers. Contemporary scholarship on the sociology of belonging stresses emotional management for example, when Nira Yuval-Davis (2011) writes: 'To carry out care work, the workers have to care—or, at least, to perform the work *as if they care*' (Yuval-Davis 2011: 186, my emphasis). Here the important part of the sentence is 'as if they care'. Care workers perform emotional labor, and the labor task is to look as if they really do care. Some Care workers may in fact be totally indifferent toward the person for whom they are caring. However, the emotional regime under which the indifferent professional carer or care worker works requires a level of emotional involvement that appears adequately legitimate; hence the need to produce external signs of caring that satisfy the client.

Care workers/care professional/close others manage their emotions. S/he can suppress sadness or melancholy and instead produce hope and happiness. In addition, the state also manages emotions. In a Nordic welfare state context, this state emotional management occurs in two ways. Firstly, the training of nurses, auxiliary nurses and certified home helpers is carried out through admissions criteria—candidates with the proper emotional disposition—and by a specific kind of training that has an emotional component. Secondly, the state manages emotions through the emotional regime within care services. The state manages the kind of emotions that are legitimate and those that are not, which is a form of emotional regulation. Hence, the state prescribes how professionals are supposed to behave when carrying out their caregiving work. Let me give an example from the Danish state discourse on the professional qualifications needed by certified home helpers, those who care for elderly people in their own homes, often visiting several times each day. The following is a description of the conduct of the home helper when taking care of patients with colostomy at home. The training manual states:

> The home-helper can provide an opportunity for the client to talk about his/her colostomy. Show a natural and positive attitude (remember that facial expressions and movements can disclose as much as words). (Socialstyrelsen 1977: 31; my translation)

Here we witness both a macro- *and* micro-management of emotions. The ideal home helper should exhibit a natural and positive attitude that involves the management of emotions at individual, institutional and state levels. In the ideal of good care, the self is disciplined, and efforts are made to suppress bodily expressions such as surprise and disgust. These potentially unwanted reactions relate to a taboo in our Western civilization over bodily emissions, and especially human waste. To remove the emissions of the body has to appear natural and caring. The home helper must *care* about emptying the colostomy bag and not reflect any disgust with the task. The ideal of care becomes a professional stance where the supposedly 'natural' behavior is constructed, and the ideal behavior is in fact a disciplining of one's emotions about human urine or stool. The care professional is regulated and disciplined by the state, and thereby the boundary between the private and the public is redrawn. What was once private (colostomy and the emotions of the home helper) enter the public sphere of state regulation.

Emotions circulate, embedded in larger contexts of emotional regimes and managed at various levels. Emotions can have many nuances and can be judged as good and bad, legitimate and illegitimate. Emotions can be suppressed or induced, and care can be seen as part of different emotional regimes in hospitals, nursing homes and private homes of elderly. Struggles can occur as care workers, carers and professional carers struggle with their feelings of inadequacy and/or of illegitimate feelings when they meet vulnerable elderly, not to mention elderly who themselves may be hostile or aggressive due to dementia or other illnesses. These struggles can take place between the person needing care and various family members trying to help, between the professional carer and the state, and/or between the professional carer/the care worker and the person requiring care. Struggles can also occur between different emotional regimes when different kinds of emotions are seen as legitimate in different regimes, such as between the ideal of good care in a hospital, the goal of which is to prepare the patient for discharge, and the ideal of good care in the home.

Conclusion

I have argued that contemporary theorizing of care poses the wrong question on the wrong theoretical terrain. Instead of thinking '*What is care?*' on the terrain of ethics, we need to redirect our thinking to the political and reframe the question as '*How are the changing conditions of care and an attention to power and struggles reframing our theorizing about care?*'

I have also argued that there is a middle position between large-scale meta-narratives and small, contextual stories limited to a particular field of care in a particular national context. By occupying this space of telling larger stories, however, we need to be continually reflective about the stories we tell—and to avoid the two pitfalls of telling either an enlightenment story or an eschatological story about care. Using Foucault's notion of critique, we can remain reflective about sociopolitical processes, their truth value, their rationale and their impact and legitimizing techniques.

So how can we theorize care? Instead of thinking of care exclusively in terms of ethics, we can more fruitfully think in terms of relatedness, assemblages, strangers and struggles between different logics of care. Relatedness refers to the instability and fragmentation characteristic of care in late-modernizing, globalizing and neo-liberalizing times. To think in terms of assemblages highlights the contingency of care, the different persons who enter and exit the network of relatedness (including strangers). As part of re-theorizing care, I also suggest that the term 'dilemma' is problematic, as it depicts conflicts as clashes between mutually exclusive principles. Instead, I would suggest reframing 'dilemmas' as a struggle between different logics over the way of doing and legitimizing care. Finally, I have argued that we need to include emotional regimes in our theorizing in order to understand the various kinds of emotions that circulate within and around care work, their management and regulation at various levels, and how different kinds of emotions produce different kinds of subjects.

Notes

1. Instead of one voice, it developed differently in the Anglo-American world compared to the Nordic countries based on two different basic schemes for understanding care (Dahl 1997) and, to an extent, also two different forms of feminism. Subsequently, there was somewhat of a convergence, but there are still important differences.
2. This way of distinguishing between different traditions is inspired by Barnes, who distinguishes between three traditions in the existing literature (Barnes 2012). I have expanded her distinction with a fourth, primarily Nordic tradition and have added some theorists to her categorizations. In their work on the political economy of care, Hoppania and Vaittinen distinguish two traditions (Hoppania and Vaittinen 2015). Others have distinguished between a first and second generation of care theorists (Beasley and Bacchi 2007; Hankivsky 2014).
3. In the 1980s, a confrontation took place between the Anglo-American and the primarily Scandinavian double perspectives. This resulted in self-reflection among both schools and some convergence (Dahl 1997).
4. It should be recalled that this is an empirical finding by Mol. There might be additional logics; e.g., we have identified three logics in contemporary elderly care (Dahl et al. 2015).

5. Care being characterized in this way also implies an increasing need for coordination.

6. It was tempting to utilize their concept of 'rhizome', but its biological associations pose an obstacle. A rhizome creates an impression of care as always being created—in one form or another, like a plant that will always emerge again. But what if this is not the case? What happens when someone is only minimally cared for or even abandoned? In that case, the biological metaphor is not useful for us trying to understand the contemporary conditions of care.I also considered the concept of a social network, a concept that has become fashionable within the social sciences, being advanced by various theorists such as Castells and Fraser (Castells 2000; Fraser 2008). Castells relates the increasing prevalence of networks to the transformation of societies in regard to the flow of information and globalization (Castells 2000). In his view, the network society is strongly related to the Information Age. Networks, however, have always existed. Castells identifies social networks as not necessarily being a part of the theory of a network society. Social networks are characteristic of 'ever shifting individuals' (Castells 2000: 21). However, 'network' is a positively valorized concept—and is used in political discourse as something desirable concerning governance. It is this valorization that I want to avoid here.

7. Here I use the concept of a stranger in a broader sense than applied by Marian Barnes, whose 'stranger' concept is limited to encounters with unknown others in the public sphere, that is, outside the home (Barnes 2012: 105–123).

8. In order to work with the concept of 'assemblage' in care, we would need to consider whether assemblage would be an analytical concept also covering institutions, discourses, logics, etc.

9. I use the concept of an emotional regime rather than relating affective labour to the 'economy' as argued by Hardt (1999). The latter is about an exchange of goods and draws too heavily on something relatively static and unavoidable, i.e. the 'economy'.

10. My goal in mentioning knowledge in relation to care work and emotions is to stress that care work does not exclusively consist of doing something connected to one or more emotions inscribed on the bodily surface. There is also a knowledge regime, as Foucault has stressed in his writings on governmentality and the relationship between professionals and the state (Foucault 1991).

References

Ahmed, S. (2004). *The cultural politics of emotion*. Edinburgh: Edinburgh University Press.

Andersson, K. (2007). *Omsorg under förhandling—Om tid, behov och kön i en föränderlig hemtjänstverksamhet*. Umeå: Institutionen för social arbete.

Andersson, K. (2012). Paradoxes of gender in elderly care: The case of men as care workers in Sweden. *NORA – Nordic Journal of Feminist and Gender Research, 20*(3), 166–181.

Arendt, H. (1986). Communicative power. In S. Lukes (Ed.), *Power*. Oxford: Blackwell.

Barnes, M. (2012). *Care in everyday life—An ethic of care in practice*. Bristol: The Policy Press.

Beasley, C., & Bacchi, C. (2007). Envisaging a new politics for an ethical future. Beyond trust, care and generosity—Towards an ethic of 'social flesh'. *Feminist Theory, 8*(3), 279–298.

Bubeck, D. (1995). *Care, gender and justice*. Oxford: Clarendon Press.

Butler, J. (1990). *Gender trouble: Feminism and the subversion of identity*. New York: Routledge.

Castells, M. (2000). Materials for an exploratory theory of the network society. *British Journal of Sociology, 5*(1), 5–24.

Cooper, D. (2007). 'Well, you go there to get off': Visiting feminist care ethics through a women's bath house. *Feminist Theory, 8*(3), 243–262.

Dahl, H. M. (1997). Mellem kærlighed og arbejde—Omsorgsteori: Traditioner og centrale temaer. *Kvinder, Køn & Forskning, 6*(2), 56–65.

Dahl, H. M. (2000). A perceptive and reflective state? *European Journal of Women's Studies, 7*(4), 475–494.

Dahl, H. M., & Rasmussen, B. (2012). Paradoxes in elder care—The Nordic model. In A. Kamp & H. Hvid (Eds.), *Elderly care in transition—Management, meaning and identity at work. A Scandinavian perspective* (pp. 29–49). Copenhagen: Copenhagen Business School Press.

Dahl, H. M., Eskelinen, L., & Hansen, E. B. (2015). Co-existing principles and logics of elder care: Help to self-help and consumer-oriented service. *International Journal of Social Welfare, 24*(3), 287–295.

Deleuze, G., & Guattari, F. (1988). *A thousand plateaus: Capitalism and schizophrenia*. London: The Athlone Press.

Emmet, D. (1953–1954). The concept of power. *Proceedings of the Aristotelian Society, 54*, 1–26.

Ferguson, K. (1987). Male-ordered politics: Feminism and political science. In T. Ball (Ed.), *Idioms of inquiry and renewal in political science* (pp. 209–229). Albany: State University of New York.

Finch, J. (1989). *Family obligations and social change.* Cambridge: Polity.

Fineman, M. A. (2008). The vulnerable subject: Anchoring equality in the human condition. *Yale Journal of Law and Feminism, 20*(1), 1–23.

Foucault, M. (1978). *The history of sexuality: An introduction.* New York: Random House.

Foucault, M. (1980). *Power/knowledge.* C. Gordon (Ed.). New York: Random House.

Foucault, M. (1991). Governmentality. In G. Burchell, C. Gordon, & P. Miller (Eds.), *The Foucault effect—Studies in governmentality* (pp. 87–104). Chicago: The University of Chicago Press.

Foucault, M. (1997). What is critique? In S. Lotringer & S. Hochroth (Eds.), *The politics of truth* (pp. 23–82). New York: Semiotext(e).

Fraser, N. (1997). *Justice interruptus.* New York: Routledge.

Fraser, N. (2008). *Scales of justice—Reimagining political space in a globalizing world.* Cambridge: Polity.

Gilligan, C. (1982). *In a different voice.* Cambridge, MA: Harvard University Press.

Graham, H. (1991). The concept of caring in feminist research. *Sociology, 25*(1), 507–515.

Hankivsky, O. (2014). Rethinking care ethics: On the promise and potential of an intersectional analysis. *American Political Science Review, 108*(2), 252–264.

Haraway, D. (1988). Situated knowledges: The science question in feminism and the privilege of perspective. *Feminist Studies, 14*(3), 575–599.

Hardt, M. (1999). Affective labor. *Boundary 2, 26*(2), 89–100.

Hartsock, N. (1985). *Money, sex and power.* Boston: Northeastern University Press.

Hekman, S. J. (1995). *Moral voices—Moral selves—Carol Gilligan and feminist moral theory.* University Park: Pennsylvania State University Press.

Hemmings, C. (2011). *Why stories matter—The political grammar of feminist theory.* London: Duke University Press.

Hochschild, A. R. (1983). *The managed heart: The commercialization of human feeling.* Berkeley: University of California Press.

Hochschild, A. R. (2001). Global care chains and emotional surplus value. In W. Hutton & A. Giddens (Eds.), *On the edge: Living with global capitalism* (pp. 130–146). London: Vintage.

Hochschild, A. (2003). Love and gold. In B. Ehrenreich & A. R. Hochschild (Eds.), *Global woman: Nannies, maids and sex workers in the new economy*. London: Granta Books.

Hockey, J., & James, A. (1993). *Growing up and growing old—Ageing and dependency in the life course*. London: SAGE.

Hoppania, H., & Vaittinen, T. (2015). A household full of bodies: Neoliberalism, care and 'the political'. *Global Society, 29*(1), 70–88.

Isaksen, L. W. (2007). Gender, care work and globalization: Local problems and transnational solutions in the Norwegian welfare state. In M. G. Cohen & J. Brodie (Eds.), *Remapping gender in the new global order*. New York: Routledge.

Isaksen, L. W., Devi, S. U., & Hochschild, A. R. (2008). Global care crisis: A problem of capital, care chain, or commons? *American Behavioral Scientist, 52*(3), 405–425.

Kittay, E. F., Jennings, B., & Wasunna, A. A. (2005). Dependency, difference and the global ethics of long-term care. *The Journal of Political Philosophy, 13*(4), 443–469.

Latimer, J. (2012). Home care and frail older people: Relational extension and the art of dwelling. In C. Ceci, K. Björnsdottir, & M. E. Purkis (Eds.), *Perspectives on care for older people* (pp. 35–61). Oxon: Routledge.

Legg, S. (2006). Assemblage/apparatus: Using Deleuze and Foucault. *Area, 43*(2), 128–133.

Leira, A. (1994). The concept of caring: Loving, thinking and doing. *Social Service Review, 68*(2), 185–201.

Lyotard, J. F. (1984). *The postmodern condition: A report on knowledge*. Manchester: Manchester University Press.

Mahon, R., & Robinson, F. (2011). Introduction. In R. Mahon & F. Robinson (Eds.), *Feminist ethics and social policy* (pp. 1–17). Vancouver: UBC Press.

Marcus, G. E., & Saka, E. (2006). Assemblage. *Theory, Culture & Society, 23*(2–3), 101–109.

Martinsen, K. (1994). *Fra Marx til Løgstrup: om etik og sanselighed i sygeplejen*. Copenhagen: Munksgaard.

Mol, A. (2008). *The logic of care—Health and the problem of patient choice*. London: Routledge.

Noddings, N. (1984). *Caring: A feminine approach to ethics and moral education*. Berkeley: University of California Press.

Parrenas, R. S. (2001). Mothering from a distance: Emotions, gender, and intergenerational relations in Filipino transnational families. *Feminist Studies, 27*(2), 361.

Robinson, F. (1999). *Globalizing care – Ethics, Feminist theory and international relations*. Boulder: Westview Press.

Rogers, A. C. (1997). Vulnerability, health and health care. *Journal of Advanced Nursing, 26*, 65–72.

Sarvasy, W., & Longo, P. (2004). The globalization of care—Kant's world citizenship and Filipina migrant domestic workers. *International Feminist Journal of Politics, 6*(3), 392–415.

Socialstyrelsen. (1977). *Undervisningsvejledning—overgangskursus (2 ugers grundkursus) for hjemmehjælpere*. København: Socialstyrelsen.

Spanger, M., & Dahl, H. M. (2010). 'Sex-workers' transnational and local motherhood: Presence and/or absence? In L. W. Isaksen (Ed.), *Global care work—Gender and migration in Nordic countries* (pp. 117–136). Lund: Nordic Academic Press.

Spanger, M., Dahl, H. M., & Petterson, E. (manuscript). How do states condition care chains? Discursive framings, heterogeneous states and multi-level governance.

Stone, D. (2000). Caring by the book. In M. H. Meyer (Ed.), *Care work, gender, labour and the welfare state* (pp. 89–111). London: Routledge.

Thomas, C. (1993). De-constructing concepts of care. *Sociology, 27*(4), 649–669.

Tronto, J. (1993). *Moral boundaries*. New York: Routledge.

Tronto, J. (2010). Creating caring institutions: Politics, plurality and purpose. *Ethics & Social Welfare, 4*(2), 158–171.

Tronto, J. (2011). Privatizing neo-colonialism; migrant domestic care workers, partial citizenship and responsibility. In H. M. Dahl, M. Keränen, & A. Kovalainen (Eds.), *Europeanization, care and gender—Global complexities* (pp. 165–181). Basingstoke: Palgrave Macmillan.

Tronto, J. (2013). *Caring democracy—Markets, equality and justice*. New York: New York University Press.

Tufte, P., & Dahl, H. M. (2016). Navigating the field of temporally framed care: Time logics, temporal dilemmas and processes of navigation in the Danish home care sector. *Sociology of Health and Illness, 38*(1), 109–122.

Wærness, K. (1980). Omsorgen som lönarbete. *Kvinnovetenskaplig tidsskrift, 1*, 6–17.

Wærness, K. (1982). *Kvinneperspektiver på socialpolitikken*. Oslo: Universitetsforlaget.

Wærness, K. (1987). On the rationality of caring. In A. S. Sassoon (Ed.), *Women and the state* (pp. 207–234). London: Hutchinson.

Weber, M. (1921). *Wirtschaft und gesellschaft*. Tübingen: J.C.B. Mohr.

Widerberg, K. (2007). Køn og samfund. In H. Andersen & L. B. Kaspersen (Eds.), *Klassiske og moderne samfundsteori* (pp. 597–624). Copenhagen: Hans Reitzels Publishers.

Williams, F. (2010). *Claiming and framing in the making of care policies: The recognition and redistribution of care.* Paper presented at 5th International Careers Conference, 8–11th of July, Royal Armouries, Leeds.

Williams, F. (2011). Care, migration and citizenship: Migration and home-based care in Europe. In H. M. Dahl, M. Keränen, & A. Kovalainen (Eds.), *Europeanization, care and gender—Global complexities* (pp. 41–58). Basingstoke: Palgrave Macmillan.

Wittgenstein, L. (1989). *Om vished.* Århus: Philosophia.

Yeates, N. (2009). *Globalizing care economies and migrant Workers.* Basingstoke: Palgrave Macmillan.

Yuval-Davis, N. (2011). *The politics of belonging—Intersectional contestations.* London: SAGE.

4

Silences That Matter

'Silences—Why should we bother to investigate silences?' Let me give an example of why we need to be interested in silence. In the Danish media, a new metaphor was introduced in 2007 referring to recruitment problems within the social care service sector: the shortage of 'hands-on' social service caregivers is referred to as a shortage of 'warm hands' (Ritzaus Bureau 2007a, 2007b). 'Warm hands' is a literal translation of a Danish term and below is an example of its use:

> Twenty-five municipalities inform us that the distribution between cold and warm hands is unchanged....Two municipalities inform us that there are fewer warm hands, whereas only ten municipalities have increased the number of employees having a direct contact with elderly people. (Ritzaus 2007b, my translation)

This quotation is from Ritzaus, a media house, which phoned the municipalities in Denmark inquiring about personnel in elderly care. In the quotation, there is a contrast between those 'employees having a direct contact with elderly people' versus the 'cold hands', who are managers and administrative personnel not having this contact. The 'warm hands' metaphor is neither neutral in its lived effects nor is it generated

.n a vacuum.[1] 'Warm hands' was generated in a Western context stressing the practical aspects of care (the number of employees), that of doing and helping somebody with the body, and the affective aspects that 'warmth' connotes. It is about doing care in a particular way—bodily close—with positive investments of emotions—warmth. This kind of metaphor is what I earlier identified as being indicative of an 'emotional regime'. An emotional regime that uses the concept of 'warm hands' is not only stressing the practical aspects of care, it is simultaneously silencing the cognitive aspect of care, that is, the knowledge base needed to carry out proper care. Several forms of knowledge are silenced when using the 'warm hands' metaphor. Both the scientific knowledge required to help an Alzheimer's patient, to detect signs of diabetes, and the experience-based knowledge about a particular elderly and his/her pattern of behavior in relation to the sickness. 'Warm hands' is enabled by a particular discourse and reproduces it by making care 'something anybody can do', since it is just a question of 'hands'. However, by specifying that the hands must be 'warm', the concept is coded in a feminine way by playing on the caring/warm versus non-caring/cold dichotomy. The metaphor thus generates an identity between 'woman' and 'warm hands'. This media discourse illustrates how a politicization and framing of care in a particular way takes place, thereby silencing some elements of care. Silence matters. And we can gain important insights about both power and subalternity by studying how silencing takes place. This example was from the media discourse, however from now on there will be a focus upon the political-administrative discourse which is the discourse used and advocated by politicians, managers and those civil servants administering the care sector.

Prior to the onset of the second wave of feminism—the feminist movement of the 1970s and 1980s—care was not viewed as a political issue in Western countries, with the notable exception of the Nordic welfare states. Feminism and other social forces pushed for putting care on the public agenda, enabling married/co-habiting women with children to have paid employment—and for bringing the issue of care into the research agenda and developing new analytical concepts. As argued in Chap. 3, the founding fathers of social science, such as Max Weber and Karl Marx, had not much to say about care. Since then, care is no longer silenced *en toto*, as different forms and parts of care have entered the social sphere. Much has changed. Some states have expanded elderly care in response to the so-called 'demographic time bomb', whereas others have retrenched and outsourced care to private actors or families, inspired by neo-liberal discourses and austerity politics (Ranci and Pavolini, 2011). Parts of care have become waged, managed and governed by the state, and professionalized in various welfare contexts.

Silence is not a new theme in feminist theory and philosophy (Haug 1987; Irigaray 1979; Whitford 1991). Attempts to overcome silence have always been part of feminist struggles, from Virginia Woolf to contemporary feminists like Caitlin Morgan. Silence has also been discussed in philosophy and social sciences generally (Carrette 2000; Derrida 1978; Foucault 1984; Huckin 2002). And more recently, identifying silence has become one of several stages in a feminist, discursive policy analysis Carol Bacchi (2009). However, we need to pay more attention to the dynamics of silence, its production and transformation if we are to understand how silence is related to power. Studying silence does not replace the analysis of written or spoken discourse, but is seen as a supplement to existing analytical strategies. Here I will argue that silence is often wrongly understood as an entity, as a state of affairs. Instead, I will argue that we need to focus on silencing as an active process. Hence, *silencing* instead of silence.

In this chapter, I deal with silencing processes from a post-structuralist position that foregrounds discourses. Discourses generate both potentialities and constraints. My discussion offers a theoretical and methodological perspective, but it also includes some examples of silencing in a Danish context. Like the situation in the Nordic countries in general, care in Denmark has long been part of the social sphere exciting the sphere of the 'private' and the family and becoming a societal concern. Elderly care is becoming waged, managed, governed and part of professionalizing processes. Care is the object of political debates, policy discussions and has become thoroughly politicized. Many stories can be told about the changes in care discourse, and as British sociologist Clare Hemmings has reminded us about change more generally, we need to be self-reflective about the stories we as feminists tell (Hemmings 2011). Becoming politicized is one feminist story of success, where care has left the exclusively private sphere. However, there is also another important, feminist story to be told about care: that this success has not been linear and progressive, that there have been struggles about silencing care and elements of care. Moreover, these struggles are still occurring, and in some cases even intensifying, as I have argued in the previous chapter. Silencing can occur in numerous ways, through actions, performances, speech interactions, meetings, etc. Here I will search for silencing in a single type of material, namely administrative texts and policy documents, because I deem them to be of key importance. The key question to be dealt with in this chapter is: *What characterizes silence and how can we identify silencing as a process in documents?*

This chapter is divided into five sections. The first considers the reasons to study silence and silencing, where I outline the relationship of silencing to discourse and power, and describe the dynamic element of silence, what I call 'silencing'. The second section investigates the relationship between silencing and care. In the third section, I discuss some of the analytical strategies available for identifying silencing in a synchronic perspective, whereas in the fourth section, I illustrate processes of silencing with two examples from the Danish care policy discourse. In the concluding section, I summarize my insights.

Silence and Silencing

Much has been written about the spoken and written in discourse analysis and discourse theory. There has been a tendency in discourse analysis in its various forms to stress the written and the spoken. Let us now turn our attention to that which is not stated: silence. To speak is a performative act and therefore brings particular objects and subjects into existence (Butler 1990). By labeling something, we create its existence. Without thinking and language, these subjects, objects and relationships would not exist and consequently not be visible. That's why we need an attention to silence that is, to that which is 'unthought and unsymbolized' (Whitford 1991). Thinking and language produce the terms of reference within which groups articulate their positions. Power as a productive force brings certain types of individuals and certain forms of social relationship into existence (Bacchi and Dahl 2012).

Before venturing into silence more theoretically, our investigation needs to be delimited. There exist many silences, and many forms of silencing can be studied from various epistemological perspectives. We cannot cover all of them in this chapter. Here I am concerned about silencing in discourses, and not with individual agents or interaction. All of us have experienced various forms of silencing in our everyday lives, being ignored in a discussion, intimidated by an authority figure or a group, or when we decide not to reply to an outrageous or offensive remark. In such situations, someone or several persons consciously or unreflectively silences the person. This is not the kind of silence I am concerned with in relation to care as I am concerned with more general, discursive aspects of silence. Neither am I concerned with silence related to the strategic withholding of information, such as when silence is a strategy in a social game (Huckin 2002: 348).

Silence is something that is absent, that which is not said and which cannot be said. Hence, it is not easy to detect or identify silence (Dahl 2012). An interest in silence seems to be a constitutive of our contemporary postmodern society, and perhaps even of a systemic compulsion— '*systemzwang*'—to transparency (Han 2012). An interest in silences is also an artifact of postmodern and post-structuralist theory, which pushes the boundaries of power analysis, 'interpretation' and 'representation', to the interpretation of that which is not present/the presence of absences. And although we are concerned about bringing 'things' into the light and making them transparent, we might end up creating other silences. Perhaps this systemic compulsion is doomed to fail, for not everything can become visible (Law 2007: 600). Silence points to two aspects of power: silence as normalization and silence as the forgotten/the unspeakable. In this way, silence is about dominance and about subordination. Here I will use the term 'subalternity' from the Indian literary theorist Gayatri Chakravorty Spivak (1994) to describe that which is subordinated and cannot be spoken about. Silence is about both sides of the power game.

Power as dominance is the power to name something and 'which goes without saying', such as when whiteness is the dominant norm and everything is silently related to it. Following Berg (2008: 214), these forms of analysis are concerned with 'how to articulate dominant or majority positions'. However, silence is also about the absence of power, the lack of power that manifests itself when subjects, objects, relations and spaces cannot be described and hence do not seem to exist. Being unable to speak and find the right words is a difficult position, but my analytical focus here is not upon individual abilities and social interactions but on a larger field, on what the discourse enables and prohibits.

From a post-structuralist perspective, everything is constituted relationally. Therefore, silence is not outside of discourse. Instead, silence is a constitutive feature of any discourse and therefore lies inside the discourse. In this sense, silence is a 'constitutive outside'. Any discourse presumes otherness, that which is outside. Since silence is a condition of possibility for any discourse, it becomes part of the inside, consequently attaining a constitutive character (Staten 1985). That which is outside, the silence, becomes a precondition for what is inside and hence, a part of the discourse. Silence and speaking are mutually constitutive, one cannot exist without the other, and they become interdependent. As a necessary precondition of any discourse, silence is a mechanism that allows discourses to mask or silence their own fabrication (Carrette 2000: 32–33). Silence functions alongside the discourse, or in the words of Foucault:

> Silence itself – the things one declines to say, or is forbidden to name, the discretion that is required between different speakers – is less the absolute limit of discourse, the other side from which it is separated by a strict boundary, than an element that functions alongside the things said, with them and in relation to them within over-all strategies. There is no binary division to be made between what one says and what one does not say. (Foucault 1984: 27)

From Foucault we learn that boundaries are not clear-cut between the inside and the outside, they are relationally constituted. What is outside is part of the inside, and vice versa. The inside and outside are mutually dependent, and the boundaries between them ever-changing.[2]

One problem in the silence literature is that silence is all too often understood as a distinct entity for example, implied in the phrase: 'breaking the silence'. My understanding is different. I view silence as an ongoing process, silencing. Silence, because it has to be created and reproduced, is thus an active process. It is similar to 'doing gender' or gendering (Eveline and Bacchi 2005), where a former noun 'gender' is viewed as a verb. Silencing produces the disappearance of particular objects and subjects. Silencing takes place in discourse and is not simply something that an individual agent can exercise. Traces of silencing might be left in the discourse and can be identified through meticulous work. However, silencing is not always an uncontroversial process. It can result in struggles about the silencing of care and/or specific care practices. If silencing is a process, so is speaking. Becoming speakable is not an uncontroversial process. Bringing 'something' from the unthought and unsaid within discourse—and upon which the discourse is built—into discourse, is often a process and a struggle about words and carving a space in the existing, dominant horizon.

There are many reasons to study silence, not least to expose that which goes without saying (the dominant) and to investigate the forgotten, the neglected, and the overlooked. Here I have argued that silence is not something that somehow lies outside discourse. Silence is instead a constitutive feature of the discourse, and the boundaries between the speakable and silence are dynamic. Silence, I argue here, should not be seen as an entity but as a dynamic process, the silencing that reproduces and transforms discourse into a different discourse. With these theoretical insights about silence, about the relationship between silencing, power and discourse, let us now venture into the silencing of care.

Silencing and Care

Lacking a proper language means everything. If you cannot describe it, it does not exist. The French 'postmodern feminists', as advocated by Hélène Cixous, Luce Irigaray and Julia Kristeva (Moi 1985) were concerned with the possibilities and restraints that Western discourse provided. They were occupied with the 'feminine' and its position in language, that is, whether it could be represented in language, and if so, how. Their conclusion was that the 'feminine' could only be represented in language as identity with the supposedly 'masculine' or as an aberration, that is, an opposition (Irigaray 1979; Cixous 1980; Kristeva 1991). And as discourse could not grasp and describe the 'feminine' in its complexity, language would either create a parody or silence it. Language could not represent the 'feminine' in its complexity.

These were their insights nearly three decades ago, and they are still relevant today in a related field, that of care. The insights of the postmodern feminists can give us valuable insights about the relationship between discourse and care. That, like the feminine, care can only be presented as identity with or in opposition to the dominant norm. Care becomes an aberration. On the one hand, care is different from the dominant discourse, simultaneously threatening it and being its precondition. It is in this sense that Annemarie Mol labels care a 'heterotopy' (2008), the place of the Other. Normally such a heterotopy would lie outside our Western world. But here the heterotopy is inside, as Mol argues (2008)—in our midst—complicating our usual understandings of autonomy and rationality:

> A heterotopia is a place that is *other*. It allows one to see old issues with new eyes; and to listen with strange ears to what seemed to speak for itself. This specific heterotopia, however, that of care, is not elsewhere, but within. (Mol 2008: 91)

Care becomes the radical Other, exposing our dependence and vulnerability in contrast to the dominant ideal of independence and control. This ideal derives from liberal political thought, as the American political scientist Joan Tronto has shown us (Tronto 1993). Care has become the traditionally silenced building block of our Western world. Care has become a strange paradox: it is a precondition for our civilization, but it is silenced as the Other that cannot wholly be grasped within the dominant logics.

However, when care becomes politicized, when it becomes part of political-administrative discourses, it cannot remain the place of the Other. Care becomes part of regulation and must be fitted into existing logics, where it can either conform to existing logics or become that which does not fit: non-identity. Care and care needs have to become administrable (Fraser 1989). In order to be intelligible in a political-administrative logic, care becomes reduced to identity, that is, as something that has to fit into our governing rationales of reason and control. Care is forced into a discursive straitjacket of being predictable, controllable and transparent. In this political-administrative discourse, care is seen as governable. As governable, it must be split up into sub-units and tasks (Dahl 2005). In doing so, it becomes hardly recognizable. In this way, care, like 'femininity', becomes a parody. At the same as it becomes a parody, care is simultaneously suppressed. It becomes silenced as Mol states: 'The ideal of good care is silently incorporated in practices and does not speak for itself' (Mol 2008: 2). The emotions are there, but they are silenced. They remain part of the expectations among those in need of care and of the professional carers. These expectations function as a silent standard, meaning a co-existence of two competing understandings of good care: the political-administrative discourse and the unspoken, silent discourse. In this silenced standard of care, care is associated with positive elements, such as 'doing good' and affective relatedness, and it is this understanding—expressed as 'warm hands'—that sometimes pops up in the media.

Care is alien to a Western civilization stressing independence and control—it calls our attention to that about which we do not want to be reminded of: our vulnerability, dependence and mortality. We attempt to suppress and silence this 'threat'. In Mol's words, it is a heterotopy. On the other hand, care is framed as identical to other governed 'things' and 'social objects' and as something that can be governed, and governed in a particular way; for example, splitting it up into sub-units and tasks that can be provided by different providers. In this sense, care is stretched and molded so as to fit into an existing politico-administrative logic at any time. This is a condition of possibility for care in a particular situation of power. In this sense, care becomes a parody, as the postmodern feminists argued were the situation of 'femininity'. Care becomes the impossibility of being truly represented in discourse. Parody, like heterotopy, cannot exist without an ongoing silencing of particular parts of care: that which we do not want to be reminded of, and that which we cannot articulate, or find difficult to articulate, within contemporary discourses.[3]

Identifying Silencing[4]

So far I have described silencing as Janus-faced: silencing is power/ domination, and silencing is also lack of power, that is, being subaltern. However, care is also produced in contemporary discursive sites, as not being able to say something like the 'unnoticed' above, and as a parody silencing parts of care, and framing other elements in a particular, distorting way. An important question, therefore, becomes how to identify such silencing processes. Several analytical strategies can be used to identify silencing; some of these strategies stress a diachronic approach, while others are more synchronic. Foucault has outlined two diachronic strategies, such as genealogy and archeology (1972, 1976, 1984) to discover silences, and these methods are now well-known. Diachronic strategies are not always possible, so how can an alienation be achieved if a diachronic perspective is not possible? Carol Bacchi also investigates silence in her '*What's the problem represented to be*' *(WPR)* approach (Bacchi 2009). Bacchi has developed a synchronic discursive policy analysis, where identifying silences is one out of six dimensions, beginning with identifying the policy problem. While Bacchi's approach is very useful, I will also introduce here three different synchronic approaches: deconstruction, comparative discourse analysis and memory work (Dahl 2012).

Deconstruction

Deconstruction is associated with Derrida, although he himself was skeptical toward the concept (Derrida 1988). As with Foucault, Derrida views silence as something internal to discourse; however, he is less optimistic about revealing such practices than Foucault.[5]

On one hand, deconstruction is a technique applied to the text, but at the same time, deconstruction is already taking place within the text itself. In the first case, deconstruction is an intervention into the text by the researcher (Gasché 1986: 154), a kind of double movement, where the text and its structures, dichotomies and hierarchies, are identified, dissolved and reconstructed (Dahl 2000). But deconstruction is also a movement *in the text*: 'It deconstructs it-self …. If deconstruction takes place everywhere it … takes place, where there is something' (Derrida 1988: 4). This dynamic is due to the suppression of otherness and exteriority which leaves traces within the text that it continuously tries to erase. According to Derrida, there will never be a full presence, a fully constituted totality, since essence is continuously being subverted from the *inside* (Derrida 1976, 1981; Staten 1985). Let me explain this philosophical point in more detail. Communication, the speakable, depends upon the non-speakable, silence, which consequently becomes part of being and of presence. The outside (absence) becomes a defining characteristic of the inside, wherefore the totality is subverted by the inside. The outside, therefore, becomes a condition of possibility for what is making outside and inside mutually dependent. It is that which earlier in this chapter I called a 'constitutive outside'.

Feminists such as Joan Eveline have appropriated Derrida to identify how silences operate within normative discourse to uphold masculine privilege (Eveline 1994). Developing Patai's (1983) argument about rules of relevance, Eveline redirects our gaze from disadvantage (women, femininity and femininely associated values) to the normalized and advantaged (men, masculinity and values associated with masculinity). Like Derrida, Eveline argues that 'the trace of advantage is in reference to disadvantage' (1994: 134). She suggests uncovering the silenced features of masculinist advantages through strategic interventions in texts about disadvantage, where key signifiers are substituted with opposite ones. Let me develop an example.

Some feminists write texts about battered women, women who are disadvantaged by bruises and wounds, oppression, fear and attendance at hospitals. Such a text about disadvantaged women embodies traces of advantaged men—traces that can be identified by reversing the gaze and changing words from 'women' to 'men' and from 'disadvantage' to 'advantage'. Whereas some feminists would consider why women are beaten, Patai would ask: 'How can this male privilege of violence continue?' By reversing the rules of relevance, a disruption occurs which facilitates estrangement from the familiar. Such estrangement or alienation facilitates 'sudden seeing' of the unsaid, the hidden conflict(s) and struggles over power (ibid: 148–149). By changing the gaze, we see hitherto blind spots, hidden colors and forms, and we can now understand how silences operate to establish them.

Derrida's deconstruction technique was originally a self-reflexive attitude toward Western and Westernized ways of thinking. Deconstruction is a reflexive enterprise, which considers how the normalized gaze is reproduced and can be avoided. Reflexivity consists in the rejection of a normalized gaze, it is a turn toward the traces of hidden silence(s). This reflexivity becomes more pronounced in Patai's feminist version, where the researcher asks how s/he is/has been part of normalizing processes and how this gaze can be rejected by looking at both the silenced parts and by posing the question from another position, that of how the advantaged position can be reproduced.

Comparative Discourse Analysis

Comparative discourse analysis can be used to identify 'silences' in discourse that relate to the absent (and historically suppressed or forgotten), or to interrogate the ways in which silences establish those discourses as pervasive (the dominant that is, the natural). The different approaches within comparative discourse analysis entail that reflexivity is employed in varying degrees.

Comparative discourse analysis is 'a potentially fruitful mode of empirical research' (Howarth 2005: 346). However, the comparative prerogative is often seen as self-evident (Kantola 2006) and with little direct reflection upon its perspective, preconditions and aims (Howarth 2005). The Canadian political scientist Jane Jenson (1986) was one of the first to use this technique, comparing US and French political discourses on family and gender relations. By analyzing the two discourses and the role of social agents, Jenson sought to highlight the causal importance of the national context. Focusing upon discourses rather than more specifically on the processes involved in producing what is said and not said, means that comparative discourse analysis in itself is not necessarily attentive to any form of silence.

In her book on feminism and state theory, Johanna Kantola (2006) stresses that 'comparisons reveal silences' (2006: 38). However, Kantola's focus is on who is excluded from speaking. In her methodological reflections on the implications of the choice of textual data—parliamentary debates—she explains one of the shortcomings of the comparative discourse analysis approach:

> One potential shortcoming of the approach is that it does not provide material or space for silenced discourses, as these might be too marginal to be articulated in parliament. For example, in Finland, the voices of ethnic minorities such as the Sami and Roma people, and their potential distrust of the state do not figure in these debates. (2006: 45)

Here discourses are equated with speech or communication, and in her case with a corpus of parliamentary texts. Silence becomes identified with the absent voices of marginalized groups. This view of silence as the excluded voices of the Sami contrasts with Lawrence's (2005) study, which illustrated how the discourse of citizenship limited the Sami to claiming 'minority group' status. Kantola is concerned with groups, voice and access to discourse and assumes that parliament debates are/should be representative of all the people in society. In contrast Lawrence is concerned about how the discourse, through its rules of relevance and dominant concepts like 'citizenship', enables some but not other groups to have access to a position of speaking and becoming recognized as a legitimate speaker.

The South African political theorist David Howarth (2005: 333–335) makes the case that a comparison of texts enables an alienation from one's naturalized context, through its confrontation with another, not too similar text. In this way, comparative discourse analysis can be used to identify the silences within discourses that operate to sustain taken-for-granted truths (see Rönnblom 2011: 21). Howarth offers two useful ways to reveal how silences serve as this rationalizing or justificatory mechanism: to confront a given text with another text, to confront another context or time period, or to confront a given discourse with some form of ideal 'carried to an extreme'. Let us look briefly at each of these strategies.[6]

Comparing a text from another context with what is considered to be 'obvious and natural' facilitates defamiliarization, a distancing from what is (Howarth 2005: 333). For example the Danish social scientist Jette Kofoed (2007) uses a text on social processes of inclusion and exclusion in schools to analyze a text on mediation among school pupils. Kofoed's analytical strategy, rather than focusing on similarities and differences, is to read the texts together in a strategic way. The second text is read through the prism of the first text—it is a kind of displaced reading strategy whereby the silences, such as the absence of punishment in the text, function to legitimate and authorize the discourse (Kofoed 2007).

In the absence of a comparative historical text, it is possible to use a fictitious text such as a poem or a novel to confront the established discourse. This form of comparison makes available new 'thinking vehicles'[7] for studying and identifying presences and absences. Using a fictitious text involves seeing the naturalized from another radically different position, which expands the use of comparative discourse analysis to identify silences that function to uphold existing realities. For example, could a political-administrative text be read through the thinking vehicle of a novel? In the book by a Canadian writer and former home helper, there is a short story entitled: 'To feel hunger' (Brown 1994). This story is about an elderly, terminally ill woman who is unable to eat without vomiting, and the various kind of practical, emotional and communicative work that her family, friends and home helper do in order to get her to eat just a little bit. By using this fictitious text to confront the established discourse, the researcher can potentially be estranged, that is, de-familiarized from the familiar discourse and gain new analytical insights about silencing in the story and the discourse.

Comparative discourse analysis can be applied in varying ways. Whereas some study silence as the absence of particular voices, I would like us to study silencing as a process where the discourse violently leaves something out that it simultanously a condition of possibility for the spoken. So discourse analyses can be more reflexive in some aspects and less in others; it can be less reflexive in the work of Kantola, and more reflexive on the role of the researcher, choice of comparing texts and how the reading is done in the studies of Howarth and Kofoed.

Memory Work

A third strategy for revealing silences is memory work. This technique is a distinctly feminist method developed around the German psychologist Frigga Haug (1987) and later reinterpreted by Crawford et al. (1990)

and Widerberg (1995).[8] Similar to the consciousness-raising groups of the 1970s' feminist movement, memory work is collective and transformative in nature.[9] In the words of its initiator, the method seeks out 'the un-named, the silent and the absent' (Haug 1987: 65). Memory work can identify both particular, individual silences (outside discourse) and naturalized, silencing practices (within discourse). It is, however, a demanding technique for both researcher and participants, as explained below.

Farrar (2001) distinguishes three phases of memory work, simultaneously delineating its three constitutive elements: (1) recalling and writing of subjectively significant events prompted by a mutual theme, (2) relating the memory to other memories and perhaps to theory, and (3) analyzing the written texts or recorded/transcribed narratives. 'Recalling' is a way of breaking the silence. This is facilitated through a mutual theme, such as a person's hair in relation to research on bodies and sexualization (Haug 1987), or triggers, such as a national flag, in relation to prompting memories about nationhood and gender (Jansson et al. 2008). The memories are to be described down to the last detail, even if considered irrelevant.

Memory work relies to a certain extent on relinquishing the boundary between the subject and object of research—they are one and the same (Haug 1987: 34). It requires the genesis of a group that meets regularly (Farrar 2001). In the group, individuals read their stories aloud to the others, after which each group member, in turn, expresses their opinions and ideas. In this process, the members look for similarities and differences between the stories, and try to establish linkages between them. Trying to uncover and bypass the role of the (dominant) discourse, the members are also supposed to seek out contradictions, clichés and silenced topics (Onyx and Small 2001; Berg 2008). Looking for silences is described in these terms:

> the group also examines what is not written in the memories (but that might be expected to be). Silences are sometimes eloquent pointers to issues of deep significance but are painful or particularly problematic to the author. (Onyx and Small 2001: 777)

In our terminology, this notion of 'silences' refers to the silences which have not yet been brought into the spoken discourse by the participants.

Here we see one of the exacting elements involved in applying the approach. Not only are the participants discovering their own absent voices (individually or groupwise) through memories, they are also expected to distance themselves from their own stories and those of others in order to discover what has not been said. This practice demands a high level of self-problematization by both participants and researchers. However, it also signals the potential within memory work to identify silences within discourses when attention is directed to those general practices that have been taking place within discourse that silence specific memories.

Memory work is both demanding and difficult. In an unsuccessful memory work project in Norway, for example, where the theme was 'whiteness', the researcher and the group members experienced enormous difficulties in seeing and writing about the unmarked (silenced) whiteness (Berg 2008). The discourse on whiteness was so dominant that informants and researchers lacked a common ground, that is, a shared understanding of why the silencing of whiteness is a problem (Berg 2008: 221).

The success of memory work seems to depend upon the choice of wording or the kind of triggers used to spur the remembering of the group members. Other preconditions for successful memory work are a trusting environment. If dangers in memory work, such as individualization and 'psychologization', can be avoided (Jansson et al. 2008), memory work can be a useful method for identifying silence, understood here as the participant's absent voice on a given theme (outside) and the silencing practices that lie embedded within the discourse. It remains a demanding research technique due to the time spent generating the memory, and the need to generate the requisite high level of trust and self-problematization in the group. Leaving this discussion of methods of identifying silencing, we can now show some concrete examples of silencing taking place historically and in a more contemporary context.

Silencing 'Loneliness' and the 'Professional Carer'

In the regulation of care, we can identify silencing when relations, objects and particular subjects (positions) cannot be expressed and therefore cease to exist. We begin with two examples of silencing from the governance of elderly care in Denmark that concern subjects, needs and relations that cannot (or can no longer) be told. One example is historical (diachronic), and concerns the silencing of 'loneliness'. The other is a more recent example, about the silencing of 'the professional carer' in relation to dominant discourses on marketization. By way of background, let me give a brief overview of elderly care in the Nordic countries with specific attention to Denmark.

The Nordic welfare state is typically characterized by universal social services that are tax -inanced, governed centrally by the state and administered locally by the municipality (Burau et al. 2007). The term 'universal' here means that the social services: 'are designed for all citizens, and in practice a large majority of citizens also use these benefits and services' (Anttonen 2002: 71). A core service area in the Nordic welfare state is the provision of care for the elderly. This is often supposed to be one of the embodiments of state feminism in the Nordic welfare states, and a result of the process of 'reproduction going public' (Hernes 1987). Whereas care for the elderly includes both care in larger housing facilities—for example, nursing homes—and home care, the focus of care has shifted toward a preference on providing care in the elderly's own home. This policy is codified in the slogan 'as long as possible in your own home' (Burau and Dahl 2013). Simultaneously, the state has engineered a professionalizing of care work (Dahl and Rasmussen 2012), whereby trained and certified home helpers are seen as welfare professionals with a distinctive, general knowledge and some autonomy, but not with a monopoly as in the more classical, elite professions such as physicians (Johansson 1995; Rasmussen 2001). Home helpers can be employed without any formal training, but this is not the most typical situation. Vocational schools have been created for the training of these welfare professionals. Many similarities exist in Nordic countries in elderly care concerning universalism, financing of services and their main level of administration. However, there are also differences in the Nordic countries in elderly care (Rausch 2008) and some of these differences concern the speed, extent and genesis of marketization (Meagher and Szebehely 2013).

Elderly care is governed by various levels of the state, and policies are influenced by the prevailing discourses. Such discourses articulate the current ideal of care, including those needs which are prioritized and how they should be met. Such a discourse reveals the dominant view of the elderly and the role of the state in determining what kind of care the elderly should have and how they should receive it. Discourse changes over time, reflecting the politics of need interpretation and the prevailing limits to what can be seen as administrable needs (Fraser 1989). On and off, some subject identities—or part of their needs—disappear from the discourse. Some themes disappear, others suddenly emerge as visible—for example, the notion of the elderly being 'responsible' for their own care.

Let me move to the historical example. If we study the political-administrative discourse of elderly care in Denmark using a genealogical approach, from 1943 to today, it changes substantially in various ways over time (Dahl 2000). When studied in this way, needs and identities change—and sometimes disappear. Prior to 1968, a key element in the ideal of care was to 'relieve distress' and 'relieve loneliness'. Elderly people were seen as in need of attention, friendly conversation and comfort (the Danish *hygge*/'coziness' was the word used). This theme reflected the conventional impression of the elderly as not just living alone, but also as lonely, in need of a little chat or some attention by the home helper, who could bring some joy or the 'outside world' into the elder's living room (Folketingstidende: Forhandlinger i Folketingsåret 1957–58: 2638 and 2633). After 1968, the theme of 'loneliness' disappears from the discourse. There is simply no longer any use for 'loneliness' as a word. There seems to be a process of silencing in relation to this aspect of care. More generally, the policy statements and documents reveal a move away from the negative and unpleasant aspects of being elderly ('loneliness' and 'distress'), and instead a more positive theme enters which accentuates the elder care as the provision of 'well-being' and 'enabling self-realization' (Dahl 2005). These more uplifting themes are a silencing of the negative, darker sides of growing older. Here a new road is taken. Some needs disappear out of the policy corpus, to be replaced by a wholly different, more upbeat view of the elderly: elderly care as uplifting.

For a more recent example of a process of silencing, let us take the case of the professionalization of care work (Dahl 2010). The Nordic welfare states have been involved in professionalizing care giving work based on a system of vocational education and training. The political-administrative discourse has stressed the professional aspects of these welfare occupations in terms of their 'pro-active'/'preventive' work and the 'activating' of the elderly. In the Danish discourse, this has occurred simultaneously with articulations about the autonomy of the welfare professionals, using terms such as 'self-governing groups' in the politico-administrative discourse. Together, this discourse embodies a particular ideal of their qualifications, where their identity as professional carers is stressed, as is their autonomy, within a specific form of governance. After the turn of the millennium however, this discourse begins to change. The professional home helper (that is, the certified social- and health helper) disappears from the discourse altogether. Instead, a new vocabulary is used with concepts such as 'helper', 'staff', 'implementing staff' (*'udførende personale'*), 'co-worker' and 'contractor'. Here the qualified carer disappears from the discourse, now reduced to an anonymous formally non-qualified, more nebulous staff/helper (Dahl 2010). Changing words creates new understandings and new worlds. We can speculate about a struggle between different understandings and different parts of the state, an issue to which I shall return in the next chapter. Here I will only note that it seems likely that the neo-liberal discourse of marketization, contracting out and 'freedom of choice' for the elderly consumer has created a new vocabulary and a new understanding of the welfare professionals, resulting in the silencing of some of their professional qualifications. This neo-liberal discourse of choice—see the next chapter for more detail—and contracting out has thrived alongside a discourse stressing 'the active citizen' and self-governing individuals who decide on care strategies based on their needs, preferences and financial resources (Newman and Tonkens 2011).

Based on a genealogical reading, these two examples indicate that specific identities and needs are changed and silenced as discourses evolve and change. Hence, it is no longer possible to focus on loneliness among the elderly in political and administrative discourse, nor is it possible to refer to a professional carer with the same naturalness as previously, nor is care to be seen solely as a state responsibility. The examples illustrate that professional qualifications and autonomy have become less visible and silenced. Here I have not discussed the struggles that took place prior to the silencing process. The purpose of the two illustrative examples was only to show that there is a silencing taking place, and that we can find ways to reveal it more explicitly. Clearly, we need more in-depth studies to identify traces of the specific struggles that take place in parallel with silencing processes and the logics at play that enable silencing to occur.

Conclusion

Silence is a constitutive feature of any discourse and cannot be avoided *en toto*. However, through meticulous work, we can uncover some of the silencing going on limited by our analytical focus. My attention has been focused on the silence in discourse and not the strategic withholding of information in a more agency-centered approach. Silence was shown to be an active process, as silencing. To acknowledge silencing as a condition of possibility means that we cannot make everything visible. We can, however, try to uncover some of the silencing going on in elderly care. Thinking philosophically specifically about silencing in relation to care, and taking our point of departure from Mol and the French postmodern feminists, we can see how care is both a heterotopy and a parody within existing care discourses. Care has to be manipulated, tweaked and stretched to fit into existing discourses—and in this way becomes a parody of care.

When studied at all, silences have been identified using analytical, diachronic strategies such as genealogy or archeology derived from Foucault. In this chapter, I have identified three additional synchronic analytical strategies: deconstruction, comparative discourse analysis and memory work. I have described their genesis, their different applications and some of the potential problems of these strategies. In addition, I have provided two examples from my own work: one historical example about the silencing of 'loneliness' among the elderly and a more recent example about the silencing of the carer as 'professional'. These examples show how ongoing processes of silencing occur today, affecting both those in need of care and those performing care and reframing the care discourse. In the next chapter, I will turn to more recent discourses such as New Public Management and neoliberalism—and the struggles against silencing within the state apparatus, in relation to the state and struggles more generally about the nature of regulation.

Notes

1. The effects of using this metaphor are viewed from a feminist, critical insider position *vis-à-vis* the Nordic welfare state. See the Introduction for an elaboration of my position.

2. Any discourse contains many silences. Silences form parts of discourses—and they are in the plural. But many silences exist in other fields and in other discourses, so every silence could be relevant. There exist an infinite number of silences, and an explication of silencing and power interact depends on which silences we as researchers determine are the most analytically relevant.

3. Let me provide an example from pre-school care in a recent Danish study. In Danish kindergartens various kinds of work take place in relation to children below six years. Some of it is recognized as 'professional work', whereas other work is often labeled 'practical work'. There arises a dichotomy of work types and valorization of the professional work, but there is also some work which is unspoken and goes unnoticed. This resembles the unnoticed work provided by social pedagogues. Researchers have attempted to identify this aspect and bring it into the spoken—the unnoticed is often seen as natural, banal or 'just happening' (Ahrenkiel et al. 2012, 2013). Researchers here work with informants to find words for this unnoticed work, e.g. the actions that create continuity and transition between the home of the children and the kindergarten, or the transition between the various activities in the facility.

4. This section on silencing and analytical strategies of identifying silencing has appeared in a previous version in Danish (Dahl 2012). In this work, I have benefited greatly from discussions with Professor emerita Carol Bacchi of Adelaide University.

5. This disagreement is seen in their long debate about the possibility of an archaeology of silence (Foucault 1967; Derrida 1978; Boyne 1990) beginning with Foucault's 'Preface' to *Madness and Civilization* (Foucault 1967: xiii). The debate between Foucault and Derrida is not about what constitutes internal silences; rather, it is about how difficult it is to uncover silences inside and the conditions of possibility for doing so.

6. Since Howarth does not provide specific advice on how to apply this comparative method, I draw examples from elsewhere.

7. Haraway understands 'thinking vehicles' as non-transparent, cognitive processes. They are simultaneously material processes, whereby categories can be troubled and the stabilization of meaning can be subverted (Lykke et al. 2000).
8. Although generated as a feminist method, its application is not limited to this field (Berg 2008).
9. The only exception is Widerberg (1995), who has developed memory work for individuals to use.

References

Ahrenkiel, A., et al. (2012). *Dagsinstitutionsarbejde og pædagogisk faglighed.* Frederiksberg: Frydenlund.
Ahrenkiel, A., et al. (2013). Unnoticed professional competence in day care work. *Nordic Journal of Working Life Studies, 3*(2), 79–95.
Anttonen, A. (2002). Universalism and social policy: A Nordic-feminist revaluation. *NORA, 10*(2), 71–80.
Bacchi, C. (2009). *Analysing policy: What's the problem represented to be?* Frenchs Forest: Pearson Education.
Bacchi, C., & Dahl, H. M. (2012). *Silencing—Inside/outside.* Unpublished work-in-progress.
Berg, A.-J. (2008). Silence and articulation: Whiteness, racialization and feminist memory work. *NORA, 16*(4), 213–227.
Boyne, R. (1990). *Foucault and Derrida—The other side of reason.* London/New York: Routledge.
Brown, R. (1994). At føle sult. In R. Brown (Ed.), *Kroppens gaver* (pp. 47–62). Århus: Klim.
Burau, V., & Dahl, H. M. (2013). Trajectories of change in Danish long-term care policies: Reproduction by adaptation through top-down and bottom-up reforms. In C. Ranci & E. Pavolini (Eds.), *Reforms in Long-term care policies—Investigating institutional change and social impacts* (pp. 79–96). New York: Springer.
Burau, V., et al. (2007). *Governing home care: A cross-national comparison.* Cheltenham: Edward Elgar.
Butler, J. (1990). *Gender trouble: Feminism and the subversion of identity.* New York: Routledge.

Carrette, J. R. (2000). *Foucault and religion: Spiritual corporality and political spirituality*. London: Routledge.

Cixous, H. (1980). Sorties. In E. Marks & L. Courtivron (Eds.), *New French feminisms* (pp. 90–99). Amherst: The University of Massachusetts Press.

Crawford, J., Kippax, S., Onyx, J., Gault, U., & Merton, P. (1990). *Emotion and gender: Constructing meaning from memory*. London: SAGE.

Dahl, H. M. (2000). *Fra kitler til eget tøj—Diskurser om professionalisme, omsorg og køn, Ph.D. thesis*. Århus: Politica.

Dahl, H. M. (2005). A changing ideal of care in Denmark: A different form of retrenchment? In H. M. Dahl & T. R. Eriksen (Eds.), *Dilemmas of care in the Nordic welfare state—Continuity and change* (pp. 47–61). Aldershot: Ashgate.

Dahl, H. M. (2010). Nye styringsformer og anerkendelseskamp - Den vrede hjemmehjælper? *Kvinder, Køn & Forskning, 19*(4), 19–30.

Dahl, H. M. (2012). Tavshed som magt og afmagt. *Tidsskriftet Antropologi, 33*(66), 3–16.

Dahl, H. M., & Rasmussen, B. (2012). Paradoxes in elderly care: The Nordic model. In A. Kamp & H. Hvid (Eds.), *Elderly care in transition—Management, meaning and identity at work: A Scandinavian perspective* (pp. 29–49). Copenhagen: Copenhagen Business School Press.

Derrida, J. (1976). *Of grammatology* (G. C. Spivak, Trans.). Baltimore: Johns Hopkins University Press.

Derrida, J. (1978). *Writing and difference* (A. Bass, Trans.). Chicago: The University of Chicago Press.

Derrida, J. (1981). *Disseminations* (B. Johnson, Trans.). Chicago: The University of Chicago Press.

Derrida, J. (1988). Letter to a Japanese friend. In D. Wood & R. Berbasconi (Eds.), *Derrida and différance*. Evanston: Northwestern University Press.

Eveline, J. (1994). The politics of advantage. *Australian Feminist Studies, 19*(autumn), 129–154.

Eveline, J. and Bacchi, C. (2005). What are we mainstreaming when we mainstream gender. *International Feminist Journal of Politics, 7*(4), 496–512.

Farrar, P. D. (2001). *Too painful to remember: Memory-work as a method to explore sensitive research topics*. http://epress.lib.uts.edu.au/dspace/handle/2100/414. Accessed 9 Sept 2016.

Folketingstidende: Forhandlinger i Folketingsåret 1957–58.

Foucault, M. (1967). *Madness and civilization: A history of insanity in the age of reason*. London: Routledge.

Foucault, M. (1972). *The archeology of knowledge* (6th ed.). London: Tavistock/ Routledge.

Foucault, M. (1976). Lecture one: 7 January 1976, in 'Two lectures'. In C. Gordon (Ed.), *Michel Foucault power/knowledge: Selected interviews and other writings 1972–1977 by Michel Foucault* (C. Gordon, L. Marshall, J. Mepham, & K. Soper, Trans.) (pp. 78–92). New York: Harvester Wheatsheaf.

Foucault, M. (1984 [1976]). *The history of sexuality: An introduction* (R. Hurley, Trans.). London: Penguin Books.

Fraser, N. (1989). Talking about needs: Interpretative contexts as political conflicts in welfare state societies. *Ethics, 99*, 291–313.

Gasché, R. (1986). *The tain of the mirror.* Cambridge, MA: Harvard University Press.

Han, B.-C. (2012). *Transparenzgesellschaft.* Berlin: Matthes & Seitz Verlagsgesellschaft.

Haug, F. (1987). Memory work. In F. Haug (Ed.), *Female sexualization* (pp. 29–72). London: Verso.

Hemmings, C. (2011). *Why stories matter: The political grammar of feminist theory.* London: Duke University Press.

Hernes, H. (1987). *Welfare state and woman power—Essays in state feminism.* Oslo: Universitetsforlaget.

Howarth, D. (2005). Applying discourse theory: The method of articulation. In D. Howarth & J. Torfing (Eds.), *Discourse theory in European politics: Identity, policy and governance* (pp. 316–349). Basingstoke: Palgrave Macmillan.

Huckin, T. (2002). Textual silence and the discourse of homelessness. *Discourse & Society, 13*(2), 347–372.

Irigaray, L. (1979). *Das Geschlecht, das nicht eins ist.* Berlin: Merve Verlag.

Jansson, M., Wendt, M., & Åse, C. (2008). Memory work reconsidered. *NORA, 16*(4), 228–240.

Jenson, J. (1986). Gender and reproduction: Or, babies and the state. *Studies in Political Economy, 20*(summer), 9–46.

Johansson, S. (1995). Introduktion. In S. Johansson (Ed.), *Sjukhus och hem som arbetsplats* (pp. 9–43). Stockholm: Bonniers.

Kantola, J. (2006). *Feminists theorize the state.* Basingstoke: Palgrave Macmillan.

Kofoed, J. (2007). Ansvar for egen elevhed. Suspensive komparationer på arbejde. In J. Kofoed & D. Staunæs (Eds.), *Magtballader—14 fortællinger om magt, modstand og menneskers tilblivelse* (pp. 99–121). Copenhagen: Danmarks Pædagogiske Universitetsforlag.

Kristeva, J. (1991). Kvindetid. In T. Ørum (Ed.), *Køn og moderne tider.* Århus: Tiderne skifter.

Law, J. (2007). Making a mess with method. In W. Outhwaite & S. P. Turner (Eds.), *The SAGE handbook of social science methodology* (pp. 595–605). New York: SAGE.

Lawrence, R. (2005). Sami, citizenship and non-recognition in Sweden and the European Union. In G. Cant, A. Goodall, & J. Inns (Eds.), *Discourses and silences: Indigenous peoples, risks and resistance* (pp. 103–114). Christchurch: University of Canterbury, Geography Department.

Lykke, N., Markussen, R., & Olesen, F. (2000). There are always more things going on than you thought: Methodologies as thinking technologies—interview with Donna Haraway. *Kvinder, Køn & Forskning, 9*(4), 52–60.

Meagher, G., & Szebehely, M. (2013). Four Nordic countries—Four responses to the international trend on marketisation. In G. Meagher & M. Szebehely (Eds.), *Marketisation in eldercare* (pp. 241–288). Stockholm: Department of Social Work, Stockholm University.

Moi, T. (1985). *Sexual/textual politics*. London: Methuen.

Mol, A. (2008). *The logic of care: Health and the problem of patient choice*. London: Routledge.

Newman, J., & Tonkens, E. (2011). Introduction. In J. Newman & E. Tonkens (Eds.), *Participation, responsibility and choice: Summoning the active citizen in Western European welfare states* (pp. 9–28). Amsterdam: Amsterdam University Press.

Onyx, J., & Small, J. (2001). Memory-work: The method. *Qualitative Inquiry, 7*(6), 773–786.

Patai, D. (1983). Beyond defensiveness: Feminist research strategies. *Women's Studies International Forum, 6*(2), 177–189.

Ranci, C., & Pavolini, E. (2011). Reforms in long-term care policies in Europe: An introduction. In C. Ranci & E. Pavolini (Eds.), *Reforms in long-term care policies—Investigating institutional change and social impacts* (pp. 3–22). New York: Springer.

Rasmussen, B. (2001). Corporate strategy and gendered professional identities: Reorganization and the struggle for recognition and positions. *Gender, Work & Organizations, 8*(3), 291–310.

Rausch, D. (2008). Diverging old-age care developments in Sweden and Denmark 1980–2000. *Social Policy and Administration, 42*(3), 267–287.

Ritzaus Bureau. (2007a, September 20). Varme hænder er tyske.

Ritzaus Bureau. (2007b, December 29). Ældreplejen forringet trods reform.

Rönnblom, M. (2011). Poststructural comparative politics: What to compare and how. In A. Bletsas & C. Beasley (Eds.), *Strategic interventions and exchanges: A festschrift in honour of Carol Bacchi* (pp. 121–140). Adelaide: University of Adelaide Press.

Spivak, G. C. (1994). Can the subaltern speak? In P. Wiiliams & L. Chrisman (Eds.), *Colonial discourse and post-colonial theory—A reader* (pp. 66–111). New York: Columbia University Press.

Staten, H. (1985). *Wittgenstein and Derrida*. Oxford: Basil Blackwell.

Tronto, J. (1993). *Moral boundaries: A political argument for an ethic of care*. New York: Routledge.

Widerberg, K. (1995). *Kundskabens kön—minnen, refleksioner og teori*. Stockholm: Norstedts publishers.

Whitford, M. (1991). *Luce Irigaray: Philosophy in the feminine*. London: Routledge.

5

Regulating Elderly Care
And Struggles

Another of the key sites of struggle is the political regulation of care. Studying regulation means redirecting our gaze toward the state, not because it is the only regulator of care but because the state is one of the key sites of regulation. A variety of concepts have been used within political science to refer to the changing conditions and character of ruling, terms such as 'government', 'governance' and 'governmentality'. The sheer number of new concepts points to disagreements within this contemporary discussion about the changing character of regulation. In this chapter, I will discuss regulation in a broad, meta-theoretical sense, referring to the use of power in the contemporary context—and I will consider how this more general discussion relates to the specific field of elderly care.

Within early feminist research, political regulation has been seen as different from and even antithetical to care (Wærness 1987). Wærness regarded political regulation as embodying a different (and instrumental) rationality, foreign to the rationality of caring. By stressing the specificity of care, Wærness contributed to naming a new (hitherto not seen) kind of behavior. Care was work, as was positioned on the scientific agenda as a kind of work. Unfortunately, Wærness simultaneously homogenized and idealized care, while demonizing its political regulation. In fact,

© The Author(s) 2017
H.M. Dahl, *Struggles In (Elderly) Care*,
DOI 10.1057/978-1-137-57761-0_5

regulation cannot be avoided, as care has been politicized. Hence, we have a proliferation of discourses on the nature of care and care policy. And not only have we seen a proliferation of discourse on care, but also an intensification of the *will to regulate*, especially in the area of elder care. At the national level, there is an increasing number of hard and soft law measures and reports written by civil servants and experts that serve as inspiration for municipalities (Dahl 2000).

Analytically, we can distinguish between struggles about the means of ruling and its content. Some struggles are currently played out between different discourses about the way of regulating care (*how to govern care?*); they are struggles about the standards of care versus autonomy of the professional/the care worker. However, there are also different kinds of struggles that more explicitly concern the content of care (*what is care?*) that is, struggles over the boundaries of care needs and the kind of recipients that should be eligible. Both kinds of struggles directly and indirectly concern how care is viewed and delimited. In subtle ways, both kinds of struggles reflect competing understandings of the political problem concerning elderly care and the solutions seen to the problem(s).

Different ways of seeing the problem in elderly care exist, ranging from a care crisis, the financial burden of demographic aging, the work conditions of care professionals and insufficient quality of care. Each of these ways of constructing the problem (Bacchi 2009; Dahl 2000) points toward a specific solution, that is, how the social and political problem of elderly care, as envisioned in a specific way, can be eased or solved. Hence, some experts and decision-makers advocate using more resources, others argue in favor of marketization, while still others call for reablement and rehabilitation to reduce costs in elderly care—and enable healthy, active lives. Finally, others argue in favor of innovation and welfare technologies as solutions to the problem of elder care. Clearly, some of these solutions are in conflict with each other, and themselves generate and reflect struggles in the care field. Needless to say, the two analytical dimensions, the form of regulation and the content of care are often difficult to disentangle in specific struggles.

In order to understand the important features of regulation today, we need to understand that there has *not* been a unilateral move from one form of regulation to another. Instead, different forms of regulation coexist in hybridity, and we can gain further insights about the form of regulation by introducing the theoretical perspectives of governmentality and multilevel governance. Governmentality is a theorization about the state that embodies both an analytic of the state and a historical thesis about its development in relation to its knowledge apparatus, that is, a particular form of governing subjects in new ways through expertise such as argued by Foucault (1991). Multilevel governance is about the various levels of the state: local (subnational), national and the transnational or supranational. Governance today compels us to look beyond the nation state container (Fraser 2008) and to consider potential conflicts occurring simultaneously between different levels about who is to rule and about what, struggles over the most effective policy instruments and new ideas about care that travel globally without it always being possible to identify the genesis of the ideas (Dahl et al. 2015a). We also witness the intensifying role of global actors such as the OECD and WHO, where policy instruments and frames of understanding policy problems diffuse from these international institutions into various national policy contexts (Marcussen 2002; Sahlin-Andersson 2002; Kildal and Nilssen 2013). Hence, in this chapter, I address the question: *How can we understand the regulation of care today, and which struggles concerning the regulation of care can we identify?*

The rule of elderly care—and care—today can only be analyzed if we consider the hybrid nature of regulation, the way multilevel governance takes place simultaneously with global governmentalizing, and the fact that regulation is gendered.[1] Therefore, the next section of this chapter discusses the hybridity of regulation followed by a section on strugggles in hybrid forms of regulation. In the section "Multilevel, Global Governmentality" I highlight multilevel, global governmentality aspects of caregiving and thereafter provide examples of the tensions and struggles related to this characteristic of regulation. In the section "Gendered Regulation" I describe the gendered aspects of regulation followed with a section "Struggles about gendered regulation" giving examples of tensions and struggles within this mode of regulation. In the final section, I offer conclusions about changes in the nature of regulation in care.

From Government to Hybrid Forms of Regulation

Regulating care is not neutral. It matters how care is ruled, as it shapes our understandings of ourselves and our responsibilities. Thus, any form of regulation creates a specific way of seeing the social world, a framework of political obligations and an understanding about the roles and responsibilities of social agents. Are the elderly rights-bearing citizens, for whom care is a social good? Or are they freely choosing consumers looking for care as a service offering? Are home helpers knowledgeable professionals, or are they just 'care workers' performing a simple service at the most affordable price? There are several logics and images operating in the field of elderly care, but the examples above are illustrations of the way that different images create different social worlds.

Earlier, I mentioned that there is no unilateral move in one specific direction of regulation. Instead, the picture is messy and difficult to pin down. However, we can identify a move away from government through bureaucracy to a complex, hybrid form of regulation, that is, a movement from a bureaucratic way of regulating envisioned as an ideal by Weber (1921). As mentioned in Chap. 2 Weber saw bureaucracy as superior to other forms of ruling, as bureaucracy ensured that decisions were based upon abstract rules, predictability and expertise. This does not mean that bureaucracy, in this organization as administration, has become obsolete and replaced by other forms of rule. Rather, it means that new forms of ruling have been introduced alongside—and thereby also to some extent reduce—the bureaucratic one. The Weberian ideal type of a bureaucracy included a norm of emotional disinterestedness as a shield against personal preferences and arbitrariness. So instead of making grand statements about a move toward one specific form of regulation, it is more appropriate to view the situation today as one of regulatory *hybridity* that is, of several co-existing forms of regulation (Christensen 2012; Dahl 2015).

An example of the persistence of a bureaucratic rationality is the ban on receiving gifts for civil servants. Professionals and care workers employed by the state or financed by the state (via contracting with companies or non-profit organizations) are not permitted to receive gifts freely offered to them by their elderly clients, as this would be seen as a form of bribery within the bureaucratic rationality, possibly ending in preferential treatment of those giving gifts versus those who do not. Another example is the assessment process involved in all of the Nordic countries, which governs the extent to which an elderly person is eligible for a specific kind of care. Welfare professionals use guidelines and categories to assess the levels of care necessary to provide a just assessment based upon objectively assessed needs rather than personal preferences or sympathies.[2]

Another form of regulation considered to be inspired by neoliberalism, was introduced in the late 1980s.[3] Neoliberalism is often used as a broad, elusive and at times inconsistent concept (Larner 2000; Venogopal 2015). However, key concepts within the social sciences are 'essentially contested concepts' and are part a field of struggle. Key concepts invariably lack adequate definitions, as struggles about their meaning lie at the core of the discipline(s). Just think about concepts such as 'power', 'democracy', 'justice', 'gender' and 'class'. All are in some way contested concepts (Lukes 1974; Venogopal 2015: 7). I use 'neoliberalism', inspired by Foucault and the American political theorist Wendy Brown, as a political discourse that extends the logic of the market to all institutions and social action, redefines the state as subservient to the economy and produces calculating subjects instead of rule-abiding ones (Brown 2003).[4] I will add that neoliberalism is a dynamic discourse, changing over time and capable of being translated into various institutional contexts (Kjær and Pedersen 2001). Although neoliberalism has suffused beyond the state, my analytical attention is toward the state and its neo-liberalizing processes. The state is not seen as the center of power, but as one of several privileged discursive sites (Prado 1995). In viewing discourse as a dynamic 'entity', we need to consider processes of co-optation (Clarke and Newman 1997; Newman and Tonkens 2011), where new discursive elements are integrated into an existing discourse. To consider neoliberalism as processes of neo-liberalizing means that the boundaries of the analytical concept of neoliberalism are not given once and for all. The strength of the analytical concept, however, is that it brings together different and related developments, such as marketization, processes of self-responsibilizing and a stronger obligation for care duties assigned to the family/close others and civil society (Hoppania 2015a). Neo-liberalizing signaled a cultural revolution in the Nordic countries, reframing citizens into consumers, professionals into 'suppliers' or 'service providers' or 'staff', and care itself into a 'service' that could be made ever more efficient.

Neoliberalism—and New Public Management (NPM)—has been a transnational discourse that is transmitted, among others, through the OECD (Marcussen 2002)—something I will return to later—and translated into specific national, institutional contexts. In the Nordic welfare state context, struggles have been primarily related to two of the elements of neo-liberalizing, namely marketization and self-responsibilizing. Marketization in eldercare has taken the form of the introduction of quasi-markets; as markets were established by the public sector providers competed to gain contracts with public authorities (Andersen and Kvist 2015; Szebehely and Meagher 2013). In Denmark, marketization was seen as means of controlling spiraling care costs as well as a solution to the perceived inflexible and paternalistic nature of services (Andersen 1997; Burau et al. 2016). And marketization had to be translated into an institutional context of 'equality', a non-centralist state and an expressed concern for 'users', their 'needs' and their 'self-determination' (Burau et al. 2016; Ældrekommissionen 1980–82).

The second part of neo-liberalizing in the Nordic countries, self-responsibilizing, refers to a new ideal of the individual. In this ideal, the individual is thought to take upon her/himself a moral obligation to take (more) responsibility for their own lives, even in difficult circumstances of unemployment or illness (Muehlebach 2012: 38). The family or the citizen is supposed to take responsibility, for example, for care in the family and/or for the community. In this optic, the elderly are seen to have a moral obligation to fight the onset of infirmity and to keep healthy and active. Instead of stressing the relatedness of care, the self-responsibility discourses stress self-care, that is, care of oneself by oneself (Foucault 1996; Dahl 2005, 2012a).[5] It brings to the forefront a new ideal of care and of the good life, where the state introduces technologies of the self— such as training at home—and in doing so disciplines the elderly into a particular form of the good life and of what it means to be a responsible citizen, a citizen who is not a 'burden' to society. The way that governmentality governs through the formation of a new ideal is aptly described in more general terms as rationalities and practices of government that generate subjects in the first place, subjectivating by invoking and legitimizing certain images of the self while excluding others' (Bröckling et al. 2010: 13).

These two forms of regulation, the bureaucratic logic and neoliberalism, are not the only ones present. Other forms of regulation, such as post-NPM and profession-based regulation, should also be mentioned. Post-NPM stresses networks and cross-sectoral cooperation (Christensen 2012; Dahl 2015)[6] whereas a profession-based regulation is based on a specific knowledge, skills and discretion (Freidson 2001).

I have outlined two principle forms of regulation and two specific ones, a matrix of four forms of regulation that create different ways of seeing the social world, different forms of political obligations and different roles of the care worker/professional/staff and the elderly/citizen/consumer. These different forms of regulation and accompanying identities coexist, but sometimes also clash. Logics can exist at different levels and at different levels of specificity. The co-existence of old logics of bureaucracy with NPM (neoliberalist) ways of thinking, as mentioned earlier, is an example of how different logics about state-financed care coexist. However, different logics also exist at the individual level—and when some of these logics are used, that is, carried forward by agents they can create tensions and struggles, as will be shown in the next section.

Struggles Between Different Logics in Hybrid Forms of Regulation

Within the last decades, the state has been shaping the landscape through neoliberalism and the introduction of NPM reforms: discourses from the market are transferred to the state to produce 'better and cheaper services'. This reform wave and new framing of the state—and its elderly care—encounters the Nordic welfare state as a specific institutional context that stresses equality and the rule of law. In this way, neoliberalism in Denmark was translated into bureaucratizing and standardizing care to ensure the rule of law—and to gain control over the content of care and the use of state funds. Neo-liberalizing elderly care meant a tightening of the political and financial control over care as well as a codification and rewriting of care (Dahl 2005, 2009).

'Rewriting care' meant the introduction of new logics and the creation of new identities for professional carers, that is, the home helpers. The rewriting of care took place through the introduction of new policy and IT tools: 'common language' and consumerism, for example, free choice between selecting care provided by the municipality, or selecting a private provider. Here let me bring in some of the results from a case study (Dahl 2009, 2010, 2012b) of how home helpers view themselves, that with which they identify, and the way they view the notion of 'good care' in their everyday practices (Dahl 2009, 2012b). We can analyze these struggles as conflicts about the delimitation of care needs and thereby also, conflicts centered on the attempt to silence parts of care and those who provide care.

The new policy and IT tool was a way of codifying care through a new political-administrative discourse (Højlund 2004). This new tool was called 'Fælles sprog' (literally translating into 'common language') which standardizes substantial parts of communication within and about elderly care in Denmark (Hansen and Vedung 2005). It thereby became possible to codify, standardize and measure care for the elderly. Codifying care was carried out in a particular way splitting up care and dividing it into functions instead of needs (Dahl 2005). A particular language was invented and Palm Pilots were introduced in the work of elderly care. All of the municipalities now use new IT tools for both assessment of needs, decisions about care packages and the control of caregivers' work routines (Hansen and Vedung 2005).

In this study, I identified three strategies among home helpers in the way they responded to neoliberalism, its introduction of common language and Palm Pilots. The three identities are the housewife, the paid worker and the professional. These three identities are abstract figures generated from the texts. An abstract figure is a methodological tool to capture the meaning of different identities in a condensed way (Søndergaard 1994). Being attentive to agency, the study showed that some home helpers disagreed with the standardization, and that some fought to keep some of the care needs in their work schedule as well as to maintain some degree of autonomy. Two of the three identities are worth taking up again: the professional and the housewife. Resistance and struggles arose to this new way of speaking about care that the common language represented. The strategies can also be seen as struggles about recognition (Dahl 2009) *and* as struggles against the standardizing and silencing of particular aspects of care. The professional was struggling with the silencing of poor quality delivered food. They disagreed with the time allocated for the elderly, who were provided with food from a 'meals on wheels' delivery only once a week. Their protest was based on a concern about the elderly having to eat old food that could possibly constitute a health hazard. They wanted to expand the availability of services, and they struggled to expand what the common language had identified and articulated as needs. They were successful in having a new item on the list of provided services: 'a snack' which was basically a shorthand for freshly made sandwiches (Dahl 2009). The home helpers applied an active stance toward the administrative and political level, and they insisted on retaining an element of care that they had control over prior to the introduction of the common language system (and meals on wheels). They fought to keep a care need ('freshly made sandwiches'), and they fought against a silencing of this need.

There was another group of home helpers to whom I have referred as 'housewives', or alternatively 'house persons', a term less likely to reproduce gendered stereotypes. The house person was applying a strategy of resignation. She accepted the common language as the official description of her work. However, she resisted and continued to perform the minor tasks, the little 'extras', in addition to the tasks described *a priori* in the standards. She arranged flowers, decorated the elderly's living room before Christmas, or fetched the box of Christmas decorations from the attic so that the elderly person could decorate herself. The house person performed the small tasks that make a dwelling into a home. Although she resisted by perpetuating her practices, she did not resist the silencing as it was carried out by the common language. No new categories or functions were added as a result of her strategy of (silent) resistance (Dahl 2009).

The common language has stirred various forms of struggles. Some care workers and care professionals struggled against the common language, arguing that as an IT tool, it was a codification of care that introduced a 'tyranny of time'. Others' fought successfully against the silencing of particular parts of care and managed to modify the standards and categories. Others did not fight, and these elements of care remain silenced, relegated to 'small things'.

It was not only new logics that were stirring struggles between professionals and the leadership. The elderly themselves were protesting when encountering a new logic. A case study investigating the relationship between help to self-help and consumerism as choice (Hansen et al. 2011; Dahl et al. 2015b) showed how reablement (in a Danish context: 'help to self-help') has become the dominant logic in the care field. This logic reflects new ways of thinking about the elderly, and of the task of the professional drawing upon discourses of the healthy and active individual (see also Dahl 2009; Dahl et al. 2015b). This new ideal of care coexists with an older logic of 'the good housewife' (the weakest one) and a newer logic, emanating from NPM, that articulates 'consumer choice' (Dahl 2009). We found that the two major logics coexisted without tension—and that this was helped by the translation of each principle into its weak version. Help to self-help is related to professional competence and judgment, while consumerism is tied to the discourse of client autonomy. When analyzing the observations, we found that in some cases, help to self-help was pressed upon the elderly at the expense of recognition of the person and their vulnerability and needs. Here the new logic of help to self-help is enforced upon a 90-year-old man activating and responsibilizing him in his self-care. The following descriptive observation, from an earlier study that I conducted with two colleagues, illustrates the dynamics of this new regime of discipline (from Dahl et al. 2015b)[7]:

> The certified home helper lets herself into the house of the married couple [she has a key]. The couple are both still in bed. The elderly man sits up and goes to the bathroom. The home helper goes with him and removes his diaper, and the man starts undressing and washing himself. The home helper assists him... He walks back to his bed and starts getting dressed with the clothes that the home helper has found for him. He waits for the home helper to find a bandage to relieve his pain...She hands him his underpants and helps him get them on. It is difficult for him to put the underpants on, so she helps him. She hands him his socks, and he tries in vain to get them on. 'It doesn't work' he says. 'Yes, yes,' says the home

helper 'you just have to pull.' Again he tries, and again he says that it does not work and that she is much better than he is at doing this. Again she shows him how to do it, and she gets a stool, upon which she rests his leg. Once again she shows him how to use both hands. Finally, he succeeds, and she hands him his trousers, and he tries to get them on. She has to help him. She guides him in getting his shoes on. She gives him his shirt and supports him in getting the shirt on. She buttons the shirt and hands him his glasses and a comb… The man has finished his breakfast and walks to the living room with his cane, exclaiming: 'I'm so tired, so tired.' She hands him the shaver and asks him to shave himself. (Hansen et al. 2011: 50, translation by HMD)[8]

As the observation shows, the home helper persuades the man to try and dress himself; however, she also performs a more subtle form of power. This is, naturally, a difficult situation, where the hope of improvement and gaining more autonomy clashes with the push to make the man more active, but there seems to be no acceptance of his exhaustion or his repeated wish to be helped. The ideal of the active citizen is once again reinforced, albeit in a context of human vulnerability.

I will now introduce another example of resistance from research on innovation in elderly care. It concerns a simple assistive technology: a 'smart' cane. A new, electronic cane for elderly living alone was introduced, but the group targeted for the innovation resisted it. The cane was interactive, that is, included a small computer and was supposed to strengthen the group feeling and motivation for walking together among a group of single elderly persons. However, the elderly argued that they were not lonely and that this was not a major problem. Instead they were afraid of falling and that nobody would come to help them if they fell. Hence, together with the innovative team, the 'cane problem' was negotiated and reframed into one of securitization—and a cane was developed that automatically sends an emergency call to the municipality or the private firm responsible for the elderly in question if the cane lies on the ground for two minutes (Ertner 2016).

Struggles against the codification and the rewriting of care needs should also be seen in relation to the professional carers' political mobilization (and struggles about recognition) that took place in 2007–2008, as mentioned in the introductory, first chapter. Here the Danish society witnessed a mobilization of professionals in elderly care, with large-scale demonstrations demanding more time to carry out proper care and demands for recognition of their status as professionals and higher salaries (Dahl 2009). As mentioned in one of the examples, there was a clash between a professional logic and the logic of bureaucracy codification—and delimiting—care functions. The professional logic drew upon a health discourse arguing that sandwiches provided by the 'meals on wheels' system were a health hazard if kept for a week in the elderly person's refrigerator. The care workers succeeded in changing the codification and established a new codified care need: 'freshly made sandwiches'. Another resistance to the new neoliberal discourse of self-responsibilizing was seen at the level of elderly. We observed how a 90-year-old man was seen to resist being 'activated' to dress himself under the rubric of 'self-help'. He repeatedly stated that he was tired, and in this sense did not want the kind of self-help care offered. Let us now move from the individual level of logics and potential struggles to the regulation of care at national and transnational levels.

Multilevel, Global Governmentality

In this section, I will outline a tentative analytical framework that combines multilevel governance with governmentality and the transnational diffusion of framings, solutions, problems and technologies within a policy field. Although the two traditions of multilevel governance and governmentality embody different philosophies of science, they are brought together under a theoretical umbrella as will be shown below.[9]

'Multilevel governance' is a concept that to a large extent stems from European scholarship. It focuses on the relationship between EU institutions and the component member states (Rönnblom 2014: 2). The concept highlights how national governments share and contest responsibility and authority with other actors, both supranational and subnational (Bache and Flinders 2004), hence the various levels of governance. A multilevel focus allows us to move beyond viewing EU-member state dynamics as one of unconstrained national sovereignty versus an all-powerful

European super state. Most analysts now agree that authority in the EU is neither completely monopolized by member state governments nor by the EU supranational institutions, but is shared, negotiated and contested between them. To make matters more complex, the authority of the EU differs in relation to the different policy fields. Formal institutions such as laws and regulations attribute authority to discourses; they officially confirm particular ways to categorize and ascribe rights and duties to different social groups, thus creating hierarchies of needs, rights and obligations (Brodin 2005).[10]

Unlike policy fields such as finance, elderly care is not part of a supranational policy field within the EU. Instead elderly care is regulated by the Open Method of Coordination (OMC), a method of dialog, coordination and benchmarking which is traditionally seen as a less authoritative form of regulation (Borras and Greve 2004).[11] Since 2004, government ministers from different member states—and different welfare regimes—have regularly met within the OMC framework to discuss long-term care issues and policies (Kildal and Nilssen 2013). OMC is also a method that progressively helps to develop existing policies and to create an 'imaginary' of a community of destiny within the EU (Haahr 2004 quoted after Dale 2004). Care regimes can be grouped as being governed by a double principle of subsidiarity (Nousiainen 2011), whereby member states and families make decisions about care. In relation to struggles, it is possible to use this analytic of multilevel governance to consider the possibility of struggles at several levels and between the levels about the power to regulate and the ideal of care.

Governmentality is a tentative and slippery concept, introduced by Foucault in some of his last lectures (Foucault 1991; Dean 1999; Lemke 2007; Bröckling et al. 2010). Lemke has even referred to governmentality as an 'indigestible meal' (Lemke 2007). There are different interpretations of what that concept refers to. The Australian political theorist Mitchel Dean refers to the core of governmentality as '*the conduct of conduct*'. Governmentality is a new, subtle, indirect form of regulation which also includes a historical thesis about the development of state power from a more direct to an indirect form of power, exercised at a distance and not so much through legislation (Dean 1999). In contrast, Bröckling, Krasman and Lemke stress the concept of 'governmentality' as an analytic and research perspective, that is, as a theoretical perspective (*not* a theory of the state) for analyzing the changes in regulation in a broad sense (2010: 11, 15). I will use governmentality stressing both the above-mentioned perspectives of it as a new meta-regulation and a new analytic. But I will also add to this new form of meta-regulation developed by of one of Foucault's interpreters, the British sociologist Terry Johnson (1995). Johnson focuses on governmentality as a new form of relationship between the state and the professions.[12] For Johnson, the professions become interdependent, as the state regulates through the professions and the professions thereby become vehicles for a social technology. Foucault describes governmentality as a series of governmental apparatuses and as a whole complex of *savoirs* (Foucault 1991: 103). This knowledge is developed in a close relationship between the state and the professions, where the professions rule in a new way, on behalf of the state and through the social technologies developed in these specific knowledge clusters.

I will here provide an example from health policy, a field closely related to that of elderly care. National Performance Indicators have been developed within selected forms of hospital treatment as part of New Public Management/neoliberalism (Rasmussen 2012). Here an interdisciplinary group of health professionals on behalf of the state—and with the state—determine the standards ('best practice' as evidence-based) for each treatment, which then determine the various targets to be achieved. Setting targets then enables the development of 'quality' through audits and the monitoring of the results (Rasmussen 2012: 35–42). This is how state officials and professionals work together to develop policy tools and standards to monitor quality at hospitals. And an example of the interdependence of the state and the professions as argued by Foucault and Johnson.

In taking a selective approach to governmentality, I have chosen two of the elements that Bröckling et al. (2010) use to characterize it as an analytical perspective: the focus upon 'govern-mentalities' and resistance. These fit perfectly with my thinking. Govern-mentalities refer to different mentalities that are identical with rationalities that again can be described as ways of arguing and legitimizing one's position. More specifically, rationalities can be defined as 'ways of thinking that render reality conceivable and thus manageable, which is to say, subject to calculation and transformation' (Bröckling et al. 2010: 11). I use of the term 'logic' as identical with the way the governmentality literature defined 'rationality' (and as argued also identical with mentalities).

Another key element in my governmentality-inspired approach is 'resistance' as already defined in the Introduction. As the feminist governmentality literature informs us, there are two kinds of resistance: resistance as the other part of power, and resistance as the oppressed discourse that has been silenced (Macleod and Duurheim 2002; Oksala 2013; Harrington 2013). Resistance is a condition of possibility for power, as it is a *sine qua non* for the exercise of power: 'Where there is power, there is resistance' (Foucault 1978: 95). For Foucault there cannot exist power without resistance as they belong together and are two sides of the same coin. But there is also a resistance that points beyond the reproduction of given discourses of care, a resistance that Foucault discusses in his essay: 'What is Critique?' (1997) referred to in the Introduction to this book. It is a resistance that reflects the perpetual question, 'how not to be governed *like that*, by that, in the name of those principles, with such and such an objective in mind and by means of such procedures, not like that, not for that, not by them' (Foucault 1997: 28). Resistance as an interruption points to the boundaries up to and beyond existing care discourses and thereby rearticulates existing discourses. Agents are not just passive recipients of discourse (Bacchi 2005; Thomas and Davies 2005). Agents also take an active stance toward the logics and meanings presented to them. Resistance can thus take many forms: inaction, stubborn persistence, dissent, counterforce, interruption or rebellion (Bröckling et al. 2010: 18–19).

'Global governmentality' (Larner and Walters 2004) is a new concept that tries to correct a bias about the nation state centeredness of governmentality studies and think the global into Foucault's notion of governmentality.[13] Global governmentality constitutes a loose theoretical space that can best be defined as

> a heading for studies which problematize the constitution, and governance of spaces beyond, between and across states. Naming itself is an act of power. Our use of the global signifies a space of nature of which

shouldn't be assumed in advance. It remains the task of empirical enquiry in any given case to determine whether the space in question is governed as 'international', 'global' or something else. (Larner and Walters 2004: 2)

The character of the 'global' element has not yet been investigated sufficiently to determine whether it is a global system as such. However, we do know that one of its characteristics is its transnational character (Fraser 2008). This notion has been used in many ways, ranging from circulation of models, mobile actors to transnational law (Conrad 2011). Here I will use 'transnational' as a traveling of problems of elderly care, solutions and technologies across national boundaries. As used here 'transnational' resembles what Christoph Conrad labels the 'circulation of models', 'traveling problems' (for example, 'health risks') and 'border crossing languages' (for example, key concepts such as 'dependency') (Conrad 2011) and create global knowledge regimes (Fraser 2008; Pedersen 2011; Harrington 2013). The Finnish researchers Perti Alasuutari and Ari Rasimus (2009) argue that the OECD, because of its high level of legitimacy, is used in Finnish policy documents to legitimize various kinds of policies, for example, economic and governance issues. And this use of OECD reports and OECD is also likely to happen in other national contexts due to its legitimacy. The traveling of discourses, however, does not mean that the diffusion of international discourses to the national level is automatic, or that it is a one-way street. Discourses can travel in both directions. OECD is an international agency with high expertise and legitimacy which actively shapes policy discourse through the development of knowledge regimes, terminologies and categories, statistical demands, standards-setting, raising of 'crucial issues', promotion of policy tools and the exchange of ideas in various forums (Marcussen 2002).

An example of a policy direction that can diffuse 'upwards', that is, from the national to the international level, is our study of Danish pre-school care that has shown the emergence of a new transnational field of knowledge, with OECD and the EU as key players (Dahl et al. 2015a). It has become of vital importance for OECD, EU and individual nation states to ensure learning and quality in preschool education and care. In our study, we investigated how the 'parents' board' became linked to 'quality' of preschool care, and how this discourse has traveled transnationally. Whereas the 'quality' concept is part of the transnational neoliberal discourse, the idea and practice of parents' boards stems from a Nordic tradition of local autonomy and self-governance. Parents' boards were already proposed in Denmark in 1981 and introduced by law in all preschools in 1992. The Danish discourse has traveled beyond the national boundaries and has become rearticulated and co-opted into the transnational quality discourse. Here quality of child care is to be ensured by, among other measures, the participation of parents, for example, the parents' board (Dahl et al. 2015a: 231–243) through their voice and knowledge of their children and the practice of their kindergarten.

Elderly care is regulated in a new way through various levels of regulation, although some of these levels are not new. This multilevel governmentality consists of the nation state, the subnational (for example, municipalities in the Nordic countries and Länder in Germany), the supranational (EU through jurisdiction) and the international level through cooperation within the EU (the gradual intensification of the OMC) (Conrad 2011), the OECD and the UN system. This governance *beyond, between and across* nation states is beginning to form the contours of a more global governmentality of elderly care, where transnational discourses on what 'the problems of elderly care' are and their solutions travel globally and where we witness 'migratory practices' (Ong 2007). This traveling is not a one-way-street as the above-mentioned example from the Danish preschool system illustrates. Here the transnational notion of 'quality' travels out of Denmark, and is co-opted and re-transmitted as part of existing discourses of 'local autonomy' and 'self-governance'. We can thus identify various sources of input to transnational discourses, including nation states and the new fields of knowledge created. As I have stressed, it becomes pivotal to empirically investigate and identify the logics at play in elderly care and the kinds of resistance exercised. Let me now venture into the way multilevel and global governmentality can create tensions and struggles.

Struggles in Multilevel, Global Governmentality

Tensions at different levels of multilevel governance (subnational, national and international) can arise about the power to regulate. In addition, disagreements on solutions proffered to deal with the 'elder burden' can create potential struggles.

Disagreements and struggles are also likely to be generated when the positive spirit of the EU encounters the Nordic welfare model, with its state-engineered professionalization of elderly care. Recently, the EU has supported a small-scale project called the 'European Care Certificate' (ECC) creating a certification regime for entry level employees to work as paid carers in private homes (https://innoserv.philnoug.com/content/unified-approach-care-certificate-entry-level-staff-%E2%80%93-european-care-certificate). Here the EU is setting up the standardization of care qualifications at a level which conflicts with the care qualifications required in a Nordic context to perform the same kind of care. Despite the laudable goals of ECC, it is likely to generate struggles about the minimum requirements for elderly care in domiciliary settings—struggles between different welfare systems concerning the role of knowledge and the proper values in providing good care (Interview 2013).

At the subnational level—as we saw in the previous section—there can arise resistance and local struggles concerning the use of particular policy tools and principles, for example, 'common language' and 'help to self-help' in care for elderly in their own homes. In nursing homes as well there can be struggles at the individual level (Kofod 2012). In a case study investigating the roles of the professional staff in a nursing home setting, the researcher encountered an elderly woman who was viewed by staff as an unwilling and cumbersome person. The woman, named Ulla and suffering from dementia, repeatedly resisted the carer's attempts to 'activate' her through the principle of 'help to self-help' (Kofod 2012: 225–227). 'Help to self-help' is a national principle about the way to perform care, and the most important element in the professional identity of the care workers and how they should carry out their jobs in the homes of elderly. This work priority has recently been reinforced through 'everyday rehabilitation'[14] becoming obligatory for Danish municipalities and thereby for the professional carers (Serviceloven 2015).

Faced with these new 'self-help' and 'activation' requests, the elderly, whether in their own homes or in nursing homes, can resist the discourses of activation. However, between the state and the municipalities there are also struggles over the proper way of regulating elderly care (Dahl 2012b: 147). A self-reflection concerning the suitability of NPM and its detailed form of governance arises, as can be seen from the following quotation from a Commission report where representatives of various municipalities and their interest organization collaborated:

> [T]he municipalities point out that one of the negative consequences of process regulation in elderly care is that the many formal demands have a tendency to redirect the attention of the employee from results towards the observance of rules in the process. (Finansministeriet 2005: 83)

Instead of focusing upon the elderly, the quotation highlights the fact that the professional carers are more concerned with observing rules and processes and find themselves forced to turn away from the needs and the wishes of the elderly. This kind of process regulation is seen as detrimental for the quality of the care by the municipalities. Naturally, this struggle is also about the autonomy of the municipality *vis-à-vis* the state. However, within municipalities there are also struggles as municipalities differ in their approach to the kind of neoliberal/NPM path they want to take. Danish municipalities, like the municipalities in other Nordic countries, are characterized by a considerable degree of large autonomy (Burau and Dahl 2013). Municipalities differ in strategies and can translate NPM-inspired ideas in different ways (Dahl 2009). NPM has different faces in the various municipalities depending on the translations at play from the national to the municipal level, and the political constellation of the leadership. Whereas NPM in one municipality was translated into standardization and the logic of details, NPM was translated into self-governance in another (Dahl 2009). Self-governance was carried into practices of autonomy, team organization and flexibility, whereas in the logic of details there was hierarchical decision-making with more time spent on planning and coordination and less room for autonomy. We have no knowledge about how these different translations came about. It is possible, however, to speculate that the 'translation' of neoliberalism into two different forms in the two municipalities could certainly have taken place accompanied by struggles between the relevant actors (Dahl 2009).

Also at the national level, the Danish discourse on elderly care can be summarized as stressing everyday rehabilitation but with innovation and welfare technology. These are the current buzz words. Despite the dominance of this discourse, we find tensions and struggles about the ideal of care and how to regulate care. Struggles at the national scene can concern the kinds of problems confronting policy makers or the various solutions proffered by them. One of the policy solutions traveling around Europe at the moment is the policy instrument of marketization (Szebehely and Meagher 2013; Bureau et al. 2016). In Denmark, marketization was introduced in an attenuated form (quasi-market) in two rounds of reforms and created nationwide controversies when it was first introduced in pilot projects, during 1990–1998. By the second round of reforms, however, there was much less discussion concerning its legitimacy, and marketization became one of the established solutions to increasing costs, paternalistic administration and inflexible services (Burau et al. 2016: 6–7).[15] For marketization to become one of the acceptable solutions, however, it had to be fitted into a hostile environment of the Nordic welfare model that required standardization in order to ensure 'justice' and 'equality'. The 'market' was still a regulated market. And as standardization evolved and was translated into municipalities and into practices of home helpers, there arose a struggle about how to regulate care. These struggles concerned the recognition and flexibility of care in terms of pre-defined standards; for example, two minutes for tooth-brushing. These struggles were also about autonomy (and thereby flexibility) versus control. Concerning the ideal of care in processes of marketization, at least in Denmark, there was a tendency to silence the professional carer as someone with expertise, and instead use concepts such as 'contractors'. Silencing can mean tensions and struggles, as it implies a change in identity of those carrying out the care and also of what can be expected by the vulnerable elderly. There is also a tendency to use a concept of 'service' instead of care, thereby reframing it into a package of practical tasks to be performed and completed, with less stress on the interpersonal, relational aspects (Dahl 2012b). Marketization is but one example of how nation states are being increasingly exposed to and confronted with transnational discourses such as from the OECD, discourses that they must accept, reject, or invariably 'translate' into national and subnational policies. In this sense, there is a traveling of problem formulations, proper solutions and recommended policy instruments.

At the international level, we have little concrete knowledge about the way in which transnational discourses travel in elderly care—or for that matter of regional governmentality such as the EU. Analytically, however, we can discern several aspects that need to be considered. The EU is a site of struggles and an institution promoting particular ideals about elderly care. Several global institutions, notably the WHO and OECD, are both arenas of struggle and institutions providing problem formulations, proper solutions and proposed policy tools in this new knowledge regime. As we shall see below, there can also be tensions between the way WHO frames solutions to elderly care in contrast to the OECD or the EU. What we do know is there that there is a tendency for international organizations to become policy developers and to become involved in the marketplace of new tools to regulate elderly care.

WHO has become an important player in this new knowledge regime and imagines its role as one of 'providing leadership on global health matters' (Kildal and Nilssen 2013: 64). WHO introduced a key notion of 'active aging' in 2002 that has become the dominant discourse. For WHO, active aging is: 'the process of optimizing opportunities of health, participation and security in order to enhance quality of life as people age' (WHO 2002: 12, cited by Sanchez and Hatton-Yeo 2012: 279). WHO here stresses individual autonomy, including the social element of aging, whereby 'aging takes place within the contexts of others' (ibid.). In this sense, WHO has a broader and holistic view of 'active aging' than does OECD. The WHO frames 'active aging' as not just productive (of having elderly staying longer on the labor market) but also focusing on cultural, spiritual and civic affairs (Kildal and Nilssen 2013). As part of the UN, WHO frames 'active aging' within a human rights framework. WHO is concerned about the moral challenge of aging (the challenges posed to ensure the human rights of elderly). The WHO approach contrasts with that of the EU and OECD, who frame the elderly as a demographic challenge, the 'elder burden', a challenge to the sustainability of the welfare state (ibid.). These differences between the WHO and the EU over 'active aging' can provide tensions and an impetus for struggles within this dominant discourse.

The EU, in line with the WHO, has promoted 'active aging' through the European Year of Active Aging and Solidarity between Generations in 2012. For the EU, 'active aging' has become instrumental in solving and reducing what is seen as a current demographic challenge, that is, the aging of populations and its accompanying financial strain on welfare states and younger generations. Hence, the EU views 'active aging' as a solution to a threat to sustainability of its component welfare states. It therefore draws upon a logic of production, arguing that active aging creates opportunities for remaining longer on the labor market, thus reducing pension costs (Sanchez and Hatton-Yeo 2012: 277). However, within the EU there seem to be different, and even competing, translations of the discourse on 'active aging'. The European Commission seems to be pulling in a different direction than the European Parliament. Whereas the Parliament stresses justice in relation to the burdens and advantages for the various generations, the Commission frames active aging as a strategy to continue to have paid employment or work-related activities (Sanchez and Hatton-Yeo 2012). As the EU does not have supranational authority in elderly care, it is mainly through OMC that it functions as a site for learning, power and traveling of 'best practice' in elderly care. However, whether one considers OMC from a learning or power perspective depends on one's theoretical stance. What we do know is that the EU as an entity now increasingly highlights the importance of 'innovation' and technology in social services, including elderly care (Dahl et al. 2014; Kildal and Nilssen 2013: 68).

At the EU level, the Commission has taken a proactive role in relation to innovations in the elderly sector. The Commission has itself promoted an innovation to be used in the field of disabled and elderly care. This innovation, introduced earlier, is the ECC, which was developed through three EU funded projects. As mentioned, the ECC is a certificate issued to entry level care workers (who pass an examination) and is intended to be applied across the EU (Churchill and Giraldi 2013). Currently, 16 countries use the ECC exam, and the ECC is intended to provide formal recognition of qualifications, ensure certain care values, certify that the carer has the knowledge to work safely, and finally, to provide mobility of care workers within the EU. The Commission is here taking an active stance, paving the way for a European-wide system of social care education. As mentioned previously, the ECC is highly controversial, as it sets a much lower entry level than is currently found in the Danish/Nordic educational systems. This became clear during a focus group interview with experts and representatives from interest groups in Denmark, who were discussing a film on the ECC as an innovation (Interview 2013).

The OECD, as an organization of cooperation between governments, provides a forum for member states to share experiences and seek solutions. It has no formal authority. Instead OECD is a 'research-oriented international organization' (Mahon 2013: 150) that produces research reports and statistical indicators for comparisons. The OECD has become part of an emerging knowledge regime on elderly care, playing the role of policy developer. The OECD issues reports with titles such as 'Long-term Care for Older People' (OECD 2005), 'Help Wanted?' (OECD 2011) and 'A Good Life in Old Age?' (OECD 2013). In diffusing data and information, the OECD help governments with the challenges they believe they are facing. Simultaneously, they also help frame elderly care in a particular way, and in the way that the OECD frames problems and solutions, these become rearticulated as merely technical issues. Politically, this process tends to neutralize the issues they deal with (Mahon 2013: 152), thereby creating a dominant narrative about the problem of elderly care, including the policy instruments proposed to deal with the challenges identified. According to Kildal and Nilssen (2013: 61, 74) OECD has been mostly concerned with cost containment, cost-effectiveness ('more value for money') and coordination between different services. These are the problems that the OECD constructs in examining social services, and these are problems that are also defined at the national, for example, Danish level. In Denmark, these problems are believed to be self-evident, and in this sense become technical, devoid of political content. However, the framing and providing of policy instruments are also political acts: they silence other framings and other policy instruments.[16]

We have seen examples of struggles between professional carers and the elderly about reablement struggles within municipalities about the translation of NPM/neoliberalism, and struggles with the EU over 'active aging'. Struggles over 'active aging' have also occurred between WHO and the EU and the OECD, but nonetheless there seems to be a hegemony concerning the key elements of the solutions to the challenges of elderly care among OECD and the EU: cost containment, innovations, 'active aging' and quality. But let us now move to consider a more explicit gender perspective on the nature of multilevel and hybrid regulation.

Gendered Regulation

There is a long feminist tradition of dealing with the role of the state for example, 'the patriarchal state' (Hartman 1979; Walby 1990), the 'potentially women-friendly state' (Hernes 1987) and 'state feminism' (Outshoorn and Kantola 2007). The traditional feminist view of considering regulation has been to analyze the 'women in government' (Brush 2003: 75), an approach centering on the so-called biological gender of the decision-makers: politicians, bureaucrats, interest organizations, etc. The role of feminists in bureaucracy (men and women) has also been discussed, employing the concept of 'femocrats'. And there has also been a long tradition of investigating the character of social policies in relation to feminist issues (Fraser and Gordon 1994; Lewis 1997). Nevertheless, the relationship between the state and elderly care from a feminist perspective was not on the minds of the earlier feminist scholars. The Norwegian sociologist Kari Wærness was an exception here, being the first to investigate and theorize the relationship between women and the state in elderly care (Wærness 1987). We now have the beginning of research on this issue, focusing on women and gender in the care field (Hoppania 2015b; Dahl 2009, 2010, 2012b; Ulmanen 2012).

However, in taking a feminist view I am not exclusively concerned about 'men' and 'women'. Nor am I concerned with the state en toto. I am concerned only with the specific policy and knowledge field of elderly care.[17] Nor am I concerned with the way that states and social policies position and produce masculinity and femininity (Brush 2003: 52). Specifically, this means analyzing whether regulation exacerbates or minimizes gender differences in the way they regard elderly women's needs for help in contrast to the way they might 'reward' or overlook men for their inactivity in housekeeping matters.[18]

Instead I am interested in investigating gendered regulation. Here I take my point of departure in what Lisa D. Brush has called the '*the gender of governance*'. 'Gender' here refers *indirectly* to the way a gendered bias can operate: 'the variable degree to which assumptions about masculinity and femininity, male privilege and female penalty, structure the logic, determine the personnel, influence the budget, and otherwise organize the institutions and practices of states and social policies' (Brush 2003: 19–20). Brush later elaborates on the gender of governance, where she refers to the private-public split, the 'definition of work' (Brush 2003: 93) and the '"masculinist" assumptions about professionalism, bureaucracy or power' (Brush 2003: 91). Gendered regulation refers to *indirect* gendering, as it occurs in the way dichotomies and hierarchies are created concerning work vs. non-work, public responsibility vs. private responsibility and the professional vs. unprofessional. Here I am also inspired by the French post-feminists Irigaray (1979, 1994) and Cixous (1980) and their insights concerning this indirect, subtle form of gender bias—potentially—at work in binaries and hierarchies as also argued in Chap. 4. Gendered regulation also includes the silencing of gender and its relevance, and it includes the silencing of aspects of care or that which belongs to the given, natural and often not valorized aspects of human existence. First, however, let me explain why studying dichotomies are so important for feminists.

As I have shown earlier Irigaray and Cixous argue that the 'female' and the 'feminine' cannot be represented in language, and that it escapes representation due to the binary logic of language, that is, it can either be identical with or different from the 'male'. Due to this straitjacket, the 'female', according to Irigaray, becomes wrongly identified with the 'male' or disappears as the 'Other', it becomes that which is different and cannot be represented. According to Cixous (1980), language consists of dichotomies ordered hierarchically, whereby the 'female' always becomes secondary to the 'male', for example, such as the dichotomy between cognition and emotion. Thinking has ranked higher than emotions in the heritage of the Enlightenment. In the view of the two French feminists, 'the female' is something ambiguous and nearly mythical, it becomes impossible to be represented. However, their insights of dichotomies and the way there is always a priority of one pole at the expense of the other are worth remembering. This insight can be used analytically to direct attention to dichotomies and hierarchies and to the way they form our thinking. Here the argument is not that (gender-based) dichotomies are problematic *per se*.[19] Rather, it is that they need to be identified and analyzed, so that we can understand the role of masculinist assumptions. One example was elaborated in the introduction to Chap. 4. Here the use of the metaphor 'warm hands' was seen to acknowledge the practical and supposedly natural, femininely coded emotional aspects of care, whereas it simultaneously silenced other sources of knowledge coded feminine (related to the knowledge of bodies and personalities for example, the experience-based knowledge of processes of aging and sickness).

Related to the analytical attention to societal dichotomies and hierarchies is the valorization of care, an old issue in feminist research (Tronto 1993; Bubeck 1995). Another example is the dirty work involved in taking care of the emissions of the body (Dahle 2005). The stigmatization of old age, already identified by Aristotle, further reinforces such a lack of recognition (Aristotle 1987; Kirk 1995). The status of elderly care remains a problem even in the Nordic countries, with their state feminism and the supposedly potentially women-friendly (Hernes 1987) institutions. Despite state responsibility and a state-initiated professionalization of elderly care in the home, lack of recognition remains an issue, even after improvements in working conditions and wages are taken into account (Dahl 2010).

Gendered regulation is also about silencing, as introduced in Chap. 4. There has been a tradition for the silencing of gender in relation to elderly care, at least in Denmark, since the 1980s (Dahl 2000). The silencing of gender means that potential gender biases have been ignored and an androgynous discourse used as though a gender equal society had been reached. The only time gender becomes politically relevant is when the mortality and morbidity of elderly men and women is at issue (Blaakilde 2012). Not only is the relevance of gender neglected, the issue of elderly care and the distribution of obligations, tasks and recruitment is not seen as an issue of equality politics. In sum, gendered regulation is neither exclusively about men, women nor gendered subjectivities. It is about investigating the potential silencing of gender, and the way social dichotomies are at play, and the fact that some of these dichotomies are also hierarchies: they prioritize some aspects of reality over others, for example, warm versus cold, work versus (what was traditionally perceived as) non-work and scientific knowledge over knowledge of the body. Let us illustrate this situation with some examples of concrete struggles about the gendered regulation.

Struggles About Gendered Regulation

Regulations apply dichotomies and hierarchizations indirectly infused with valorizations such as masculinity and femininity. One example is the notion of 'professional' and its counterpart 'non-professional'. The professional is valued and recognized signifying expertise, whereas the non-professional, the generalist, signifies the absence of a knowledge base with its practical, tedious work. Something everybody is assumed to be able to do. Throughout history, there has been a long struggle for the recognition of care. Part of this struggle was the professionalization of care work, and another part was the recognition of care as a state responsibility. These struggles were gendered, and well documented by feminist sociology (Witz 1992; Hänsel 1992; Martinsen 1994).

There are also struggles taking place in this century about gendered regulation. In Denmark, there were large-scale mobilizations among certified home helpers and social and healthcare workers, that is, care professionals in 2007–2008 (Dahl 2009). As already mentioned in the Introduction, these care workers protested in front of the Danish parliament with slogans that reflected their struggles for recognition, and against time pressures and unreasonable working conditions. 'Time' became an important metaphor—and a signifier condensing several elements of struggles such as 'control over time' and 'controlling one's work'. They wanted more time to perform care in the homes of the elderly that is, less visits per day. They felt themselves exposed to what they called a 'tyranny of minutes' ('*minuttyranni*') in performing their work tasks and they complained that they were continuously on the move from one elderly home to the next. These struggles occurred at a conjuncture when new policy tools, embodied in terms such as 'common language' and 'free choice' were translated into the concrete work tasks of professional carers. Technologies that were part of neoliberalism were codified, rewritten and reorganized the nature of care work. The icon of this struggle was perhaps the Palm Pilot device, where every care worker had to register every task completed right down to the minute. The rewriting of care work led to the splitting up of care tasks, needs were rewritten into functions, and care was articulated as the language of practical, primarily household or nursing tasks. Tasks and needs related to the emotional and physical side of the elderly were largely silenced or relegated to the family—or taken over by the voluntary/third sector; the emotional side of care (what in Danish is called *samvær*/togetherness) was not seen as a state responsibility. The reorganization entailed more mid-level management, where planners and team leaders became more prevalent in the care delivery system. This meant less time for the front line workers given the same allocation to elderly care; more time was used for planning in contrast to exercise of care. This was experienced by care professionals and the elderly as reductions in services. Hence, there was a struggle about who had the qualifications to perform care, the valorization of care and its administrative organization for the elderly. The elderly complained of lack of service and ever-changing carers, and the carers complained of stressful work. But these complaints, individual as they are, are but symptoms of larger struggles.

These struggles can be seen as gendered struggles concerning the recognition of professional qualifications to perform care. In this sense, they are about professionalization, that is, de- or re-professionalizing care for elderly. New technologies related to neoliberalism draw indirectly upon old dichotomies of professional versus non-professional and are codifying care work as nothing but practical housework.[20] In this way, neoliberalism tends to de-professionalize care work, transforming it in the direction of pre-professional images of female care in three ways as: *housework, self-sacrifice and obligingness.*[21] However, there is an ongoing struggle between de-professionalizing rewritings and re-professionalizing. These struggles also exist within the state apparatus itself. The state is a field of struggles (Poulantzas 1978), and the state can also shape these struggles (of recognition) in important ways (Feldman 2008). The struggles within the state about re-professionalizing or de-professionalizing refer to different images of the role of care professionals and elderly that exist within different parts of the state: exchequer versus the educational/health policy fields. Whereas de-professionalizing has so far been strongest in the documentation and marketization of care, 'active aging' reframes a care worker into a professional, stressing their task to promote reablement (everyday rehabilitation) as part of their re-professionalized duties.

I will now expand upon the above-mentioned three ways of de-professionalizing that are taking place in the care field. One of the ways de-professionalization takes place is the rewriting of elderly care into mere household tasks. The codification of care for the elderly means that needs are redefined as tasks and become simple functions (Dahl 2005). There is a splitting up of the former unity of care, now divided among the certified home helper, the certified social and health assistant (a professional with more competence than a practical nurse), the medically trained nurse and the physiotherapist. The codification occurs via a particular language that stresses the tasks in a household, such as dusting, vacuuming, dishwashing, emptying the garbage and tasks related to the maintenance of the person such as brushing teeth, bathing and washing of hair. There is a codification of practical help, personal help (personal care, mental care, treatments, nutrition, etc.) and various other tasks (contact the physician, help filling out forms, etc.). These tasks become Taylorized, while other needs, those that cannot be codified, disappear, as they cannot be brought into the political-administrative language. They are silenced. The needs that are silenced were referred to as 'small things' by the home helper in the example described earlier, these were the minor tasks that were done outside the assessment, tasks which in her view were important for the quality of life for the elderly in their home (Dahl 2009). But also needs such as 'coziness' were silenced and disappeared as a 'need' in the national discourse (Dahl 2000).[22] In this sense, we witness a hollowing out of care for elderly (Dahl 2012a), where needs such as being comforted, going for a walk, small talk over a cup of coffee and fetching the Christmas decorations from the attic disappear from the catalog of functions.

A second part of de-professionalization is how the hollowing out of care works out in practice, that is, its lived effects for some professionals. Several studies point to the fact that professional carers act as a buffer between the elderly and the social service system. There is an element of self-sacrifice when this buffer function operates at the expense of the well-being of the professionals. At the same time, the emotional regime in paid, state-regulated care seems to rely on this buffer. We have seen it in Denmark, when professional carers perform 'the little extras' that are not part of the assessment (Dahl 2009) and in Norway, where home helpers reduce the negative effects of the system (that is, reduced services) by acting as a buffer (Vabö 2006). Self-sacrifice is itself gendered. It is based upon a stereotypical female image of women 'being there for others'. But this self-sacrifice creates tensions within the state. On one hand, the state relies on this self-sacrifice and the emotional work being done. On the other hand, the state does not recognize it (Dahl 2009). This tension within the state compels professional carers to formulate various strategies, for example, a cynical strategy where the professional works 'by the book', refusing or neglecting to do any 'little extras'. Using a phrase from Chap. 3, this would be a situation of emotional detachment, where the emotional regime becomes characterized as 'caring as if' (Yuval-Davis 2011). This resembles other research findings on professionals working in welfare services (Soss, Fording and Schram 2011). For example, a study of social workers in Florida showed that some caseworkers turned themselves into shields to protect their clients against the system of sanctioning involved in the welfare system. This shielding behavior had a personal cost for the social workers being a recipe for exhaustion and burnout.

A third aspect of de-professionalizing relates to consumerism and the way it stresses the wishes and priorities of older people. In a research project conducted in 2010 among front line staff in four Danish municipalities, professional carers (home helpers and certified social and health assistants) were interviewed and observed in their work and interactions with older people (Dahl et al. 2015b). Here we observed a version of consumerism that we labeled 'obliging', where the professional carer did as the client demanded. Obliging could take place in two ways: doing tasks beyond what was required in the assessment, or doing tasks in a particular way. This could create tensions, as shown in the following observation from the fieldwork:

The elderly woman...says to the care worker that she wants the mirrors polished and the tiles wiped in the bathroom. The care worker explains that this is beyond his assigned task, and the woman exclaims that she will have to employ a cleaning lady. The care worker explains that the woman can buy additional services...and that it is the municipality that regulates this, not her. Despite this, the care worker says: 'I'll do the mirrors'....The care worker then goes into the bedroom, where she polished the mirrors in the wardrobes ...and cleans the bathroom. The elderly woman is in the kitchen arranging some flowers.[23]

Here the care worker, who works for a private contractor, does something beyond her assigned duties and cleans the tiles in the bathroom. Nevertheless, the verbal exchange exposes tensions between what the elderly client wants and what the care worker is allowed to do. The care worker obliges the wishes of the elderly woman. In another example from the same research project, there is a similar kind of submissiveness: the care worker accepts the elderly person's way of doing things (cleaning in this case):

I said to her [the older woman] that I would like to start by changing the sheets because of the dust that would be whirled up. Then she watched me for a bit, and then said: 'I don't need to keep an eye on you anymore'. This was the first time, and since then there haven't been any problems. She has called the office and said she was very satisfied...now that she has finally gotten someone who cleans her house thoroughly (focus group interview with municipal care workers).[24]

Here we can identify obligingness. The home helper accepts the cleaning standards and way of doing the cleaning that the elderly woman prefers. Here consumerism can be seen to be related to pre-existing standards of 'the good housewife' cleaning in the proper way. Obligingness thus reduces the role of the assigned care tasks and the professional judgment of the carer. In effect, obligingness de-professionalizes the home helper as it is more than flexibility, it is a certain attitude.

In opposition to de-professionalizing there has also been another process that plugs into health discourses of active aging: that of re-professionalizing. When I use the term 're-professionalizing', it is due to the fact that rehabilitation and reablement in Denmark is also a return to an ideal of elderly care that became prevalent in the 1980s and 1990s with the notion of 'help to self-help' (Dahl 2000; Dahl et al. 2015b). This re-professionalization can be seen in the current transformation of elderly care, with its focus upon re-ablement and rehabilitation (Hansen and Kamp 2016). Care is rewritten from compensatory care into the retraining and rehabilitation of the elderly, the ideal being to get the elderly person involved and able to do more, to be more autonomous and independent. Rewriting compensatory care means that this form of care provision is viewed negatively, as it frames the elderly as inactive and dependent (Hansen and Kamp 2016). This transformation redirects care away from the body and its emissions. Instead, care becomes professional care, with its stress upon an analytical gaze of the home helper, who identifies the potentials for change and how to implement training. Reframing care work away from its bodily tasks and turning it into an analytical and training project changes its gendered associations from one of femininity to one of masculinity. From 'warm hands' signifying femininity to training signifying masculinity The home helper now attains a stronger professional identity with a more 'masculine' knowledge base. Her job is to motivate and help the elderly person to become more active and to lead a more autonomous life. Another process that re-professionalizes or professionalizes elderly care in a domestic setting is the de-institutionalization of care from hospitals. Needs that formerly were provided in hospital wards are now moved to the home (Allen 2012) and must be taken care of by the family and/or professionals in the home. Needs concerning medicine, monitoring blood pressure and treatment of wounds now have to be handled by professionals in the person's own home.

The two ideals of de-professionalized and re-professionalized care for the elderly coexist at individual levels and are used interchangeably by home helpers in concrete visits and during their day (Dahl et al. 2015b). However, there is a struggle about which logic and which image of the home helper is to prevail. De-professionalizing has so far been the strongest tendency, with accompanying codification in a particular discourse of housework and with lived effects such as obliging consumerism and home helpers stressing themselves by being compelled to act as a buffer between

the social service system and the anxious elderly person.
'active aging' becoming more dominant, and the develo
policy instruments such as 'everyday rehabilitation', re
has gained renewed impetus. Regulation of elderly care is gen
far as it recirculates gendered notions of work and the professiona.
notion of the professional has still retained its 'masculine' bias, meaning
that certain forms of knowledge and work related to the body are denied
professional status. The home helpers can be re-professionalized only in
a simultaneous process of de-feminization, away from housework, as the
discursive terrain is constituted at the moment.

Conclusion

The regulation of elderly care has been transformed. There is an intensification of the will to regulate, introducing new logics to the field and a
more globalized, multilevel form of regulation. When new logics encounter existing or different logics, struggles about translation can arise as
well as resistance to the encroaching new logic. Within the Danish state,
we find the two most typical forms of regulation: bureaucratizing and
neo-liberalizing, where bureaucracy frames the way neo-liberalizing is
translated into codification of tasks and marketization. Struggles arise
concerning the codification of services; for example, the freshly prepared
sandwiches being 'silenced' and replaced by 'meals on wheels'. However,
professional carers resisted this silencing and succeeded, through the use
of a health discourse, in getting the daily, freshly made sandwiches rein-
troduced into the catalog of services. Among the elderly clients themselves, there was also resistance to the neoliberal self-responsibilizing
discourse entering their homes and in nursing homes. A struggle between
the care workers and the elderly about proper care can be identified: helping the elderly in a hands-on fashion, or the more preferable guiding of
the elderly to do it all by him/herself. We witness here a difficult situation
between the hope of being able to be autonomous and the disciplining
force of the state. From a Foucauldian position, the state is in the process
of reintroducing a moral obligation to change and become autonomous
in a particular ideal of the good life.

At the various levels of regulation of elderly care, resistance is also a recurrent phenomenon. Struggles between the state and municipalities arose due to the resistance of municipalities to being regulated—and to having their care policy controlled—in a particular way. Struggles between different parts of the Danish state arose between marketization and professionalization, or put differently, between de-professionalizing and re-professionalizing. Also within the EU, there were struggles about the proper understanding of 'active aging' between the European Parliament and the European Commission. These struggles, however, were set in a context of a global regulation of elderly care, where there were minor differences between the global agenda-setters such as WHO, the OECD and the EU, but where there exists a transnational way of framing solutions as one of active aging and cost containment.

Regulation is also gendered and theorized through the lens of gendering governance, where its gendered aspects are investigated through an analytical attention to dichotomies, valorizations and silencing. The struggle over professionalizing or de-professionalizing is a strongly gendered struggle, as the professional has been modeled on traditional, elitist male professions at a particular moment in time (Witz 1992). Therefore, the struggle between professionalizing and de-professionalizing is also a gendered struggle about what it means to be a professional and which knowledge forms rank highest—or are silenced from the knowledge base of the professional carer. The gendered element of these struggles also relates to the role of housework in care (and reducing care to practical tasks), the obligingness related to free choice and marketization; and finally, the way professional carers in different national contexts found themselves being compelled to act as buffers between the social service system and the frustrated elderly. The applied strategy is often related to femininity, namely that of self-sacrifice.

Notes

1. Regulation can have different intersections e.g. racializing and gendering. However, here I analytically focus upon gendering, freezing race, ethnicity and class.

2. It's interesting to note that there has occurred a change in patients' expectations towards doctors (Obling 2012). They expect to be recognized and seen in their emotional distress and that the doctor engages in the governance of his/her own emotions. This change might be part of a more general trend related to postmodernizing and the striving for intimacy and authenticity. In this sense there is a move away from the bureaucratic ideal of disinterestedness and a longing for more emphathetic professionals.

3. Another concept often used as a synonym: 'NPM'.

4. Other feminist interpretations of governmentality exist (Oksala 2013).

5. According to Foucault, this move signifies a reorientation from a Greek to a Roman notion of care: a need for care of the self (Foucault 1996).

6. Post-NPM can be seen as a response to some of the deficiencies of NPM, e.g. pillarization.

7. Observations were conducted by a research assistant, Tina Borgen (Hansen et al. 2011).

8. This quotation has also been used in an earlier article (Dahl 2012a).

9. Governmentality springs from a post-structuralist way of thinking with a flat ontology of discourses, multilevel governance seems to operate with a more realist philosophy of science. My way of applying multilevel governance is to distinguish between discourses with more or less authority, where political-administrative discourse with a high level of authority is to be found at the various levels of multilevel governance.

10. For a further discussion of multilevel governance, see our working paper: 'How do States Condition Care Chains? Discursive Framings, Heterogeneous States and Multi-level Governance' (manuscript) by Marlene Spanger, Hanne Marlene Dahl and Elin Petterson.

11. However, the open method of coordination within the EU is one of the key sites for transnational discourses about political problems, solutions and social technologies to solve or reduce the articulated problems.

12. Here I have not entered into the debate about the genesis and relationship of welfare professions and the Nordic welfare state. For an elaboration, please consult (Bertilsson 1990; Brante 2005).

13. The American philosopher Nancy Fraser (2008: 125) introduced a similar concept which she calls 'globalizing governmentality'. Based upon a Marxian reading of the relationship between a mode of production and form of regulation, Fraser argues that a new post-Fordist form of regulation has emerged. Although I am sympathetic towards the dynamic element of 'globalizing' in her thinking as a yet unfinished process, I am skeptical of the rather homogenous, unambiguous system

of governance she paints and its causal relationship to a new mode of production.

14. 'Everyday rehabilitation' aims to 'develop, regain, keep or prevent a reduction in the functions and abilities' of the elderly (Kjellberg et al. 2011: 5) (HMD translation)

15. An interesting contrast to the Nordic welfare states is the way that marketization also became a solution in Italy, but in a different way of framing the problem. Here the policy problem was seen as one of the declining care capacities of Italian families. The solution promoted was cash-transfers to families (a form of marketization) (Burau et al. 2016).

16. A similar argument is advanced by the Finnish political theorist Hanna-Kaisa Hoppania, who argues that there is a displacement of elderly care from politics to regulation. Care becomes de-politicized such that it becomes an issue of the 'governance of care' (Hoppania 2015b: 88).

17. When new forms of regulation e.g. neoliberalizing enter a given nation state, they encounter an existing gender regime. A gender regime does not mean that it is a uniform system. It exhibits specific characteristics that can be identified when studying it and relating it comparatively to other gender regimes—and it is subject to change through struggles and changing routines.

18. Analyzing regulation also implies the consideration of the lived effects (Bacchi 2009) of the solutions pursued. The lived effects are not something that I am investigating or developing analytically.

19. As we know from the French philosopher J. Derrida, thinking and language are constituted relationally and based on dichotomies—and dichotomies favor presence over absence. This Metaphysics of Presence is a condition for thinking and communication, but the trick is, through awareness, to play with this and try to subvert them.

20. Except there was also an element of basic nursing involved in this codification (a result of the de-institutionalization of care from hospitals).

21. In my understanding of the various elements of de-professionalising, I have benefitted greatly from comments made by Tonkens and Bredewold to some of my articles (Tonkens, E., and Bredewold, F., 2015, Personal communication on e-mail).

22. Please see Chap. 4 for an elaboration of this point.

23. This quotation is cited from Dahl et al. (2015b): 293.

24. This quotation is cited from Dahl et al. (2015b): 292.

References

Aristotle. (1987). *Ethics*. London: Penguin Books.

Ældrekommissionen. (1980–82). Ældrekommissionens delrapporter: 1. delrapport (1980), 2. delrapport (1981) og 3. delrapport (1982).

Alasuutari, P., & Rasimus, A. (2009). Use of OECD in justifying policy reforms: The case of Finland. *Journal of Power, 2*(1), 89–109.

Allen, D. (2012). Bringing it all back home—The (re)domestication and de(medicalization) of care in the UK. In C. Ceci, K. Björnsdottir, & M. E. Purkis (Eds.), *Perspective on care at home for older people* (pp. 101–120). New York: Routhledge.

Andersen, N. Å. (1997). *Udlicitering—strategi og historie*. Copenhagen: Nyt fra Samfundsvidenskaberne.

Andersen, K., & Kvist, E. (2015). The neo-liberal turn and the marketization of care: The transformation of eldercare in Sweden. *European Journal of Women's Studies, 22*(3), 274–287.

Bacchi, C. (2005). Discourse, discourse everywhere: Subject 'agency' in feminist discourse methodology. *Nordic Journal of Women's Studies, 13*(3), 198–209.

Bacchi, C. (2009). *Analysing policy: What's the problem represented to be?* Sydney: Pearson Education.

Bache, I., & Flinders, M. (2004). *Multilevel governance*. Oxford Scholarship Online: 2004 doi:10.1093/0199259259.001.0001

Bertilsson, M. (1990). The welfare state, the professions and citizens. In R. Torstendal & M. Burrage (Eds.), *The formation of professions* (pp. 114–133). London: Sage.

Blaakilde, A. L. (2012). Døde mænd og syge kvinder—køn, alder og ulighed i sundhed. *Kvinder, Køn & Forskning, 21*(4), 56–63.

Borras, S., & Greve, B. (2004). Preface. *Journal of European Public Policy, 11*(2), 181–184.

Brante, T. (2005). Staten og professionerne. In T. R. Eriksen & A. M. Jørgensen (Eds.), *Professionsidentitet i forandring* (pp. 16–35). Copenhagen: Akademisk forlag.

Bröckling, U., Krasman, S., & Lemke, T. (2010). From Foucault's lectures at the Collège de France to studies of governmentality—An introduction. In U. Bröckling, S. Krasmann, & T. Lemke (Eds.), *Governmentality—Current issues and future challenges* (pp. 1–33). London: Routhledge.

Brodin, H. (2005). *Does anybody care? Public and private responsibilities in Swedish eldercare 1940–2000*. Umeå: Ekonomisk historia.

Brown, W. (2003). Neo-liberalism and the end of liberal democracy. *Theory and Event*, *7*(1). https://muse.jhu.edu/journals/theory_and_event/v007/7.1brown.html. Accessed 1 Aug 2014.

Brush, L. D. (2003). *Gender and governance*. Oxford: Alta Mira Press.

Bubeck, D. (1995). *Care, gender and justice*. Oxford: Clarendon Press.

Burau, V., & Dahl, H. M. (2013). Trajectories of change in Danish long-term care policies: Reproduction by adaptation through top-down and bottom-up reforms. In C. Ranci & E. Pavolini (Eds.), *Reforms in long-term care policies – Investigating institutional change and social impacts* (pp. 79–96). New York: Springer.

Burau, V., Zechner, M., Dahl, H. M., & Ranci, C. (2016). *The political construction of elder care markets: Comparing Denmark, Finland and Italy, Social Policy and Administration* (e-publication ahead of print). https://onlinelibrary.wiley.com/doi/10.1111/spol.12198/epdf. Accessed 21 Dec 2016.

Christensen, T. (2012). Post-NPM and changing public governance. *Meiji Journal of Political Science and Economics, 1*(2), 1–11.

Churchill, J., & Giraldi, M. (2013). *Theoretically informed case study accompanying the film European care certificate*. https://innoserv.philnoug.com/content/unified-approach-care-certificate-entry-level-staff-%E2%80%93-european-care-certificate. Accessed 23 Sept 2016.

Cixous, H. (1980). Sorties. In E. Marks & L. Courtivron (Eds.), *New French Feminisms* (pp. 90–98). Amherst: The University of Massachusetts Press.

Clarke, J., & Newman, J. (1997). *The managerial state*. London: Sage.

Conrad, C. (2011). Social policy history after the transnational turn. In P. Kettunen & K. Petersen (Eds.), *Beyond welfare state models* (pp. 218–240). Cheltenham: Edward Elgar.

Dahl, H. M. (2000). *Fra kitler til eget tøj—Diskurser om professionalisme, omsorg og køn, Ph.D. thesis*. Aarhus: Politica.

Dahl, H. M. (2005). A changing ideal of care in Denmark: A different form of retrenchment? In H. M. Dahl & T. R. Eriksen (Eds.), *Dilemmas of care in the Nordic welfare state: Continuity and change* (pp. 47–61). Aldershot: Ashgate.

Dahl, H. M. (2009). New public management, care and struggles about recognition. *Critical Social Policy, 29*(4), 634–654.

Dahl, H. M. (2010). An old map of state feminism and an insufficient recognition of care. *NORA—Nordic Journal of Feminist and Gender Research, 18*(3), 152–166.

Dahl, H. M. (2012a). Neoliberalism meets the Nordic welfare state—Gaps and silences. *NORA, 20*(4), 283–288.

Dahl, H. M. (2012b). Who can be against quality? A new story about home-based care: NPM and governmentality. In C. Ceci, K. Björnsdottir, & M. E. Purkis (Eds.), *Perspectives on care at home for older people* (pp. 139–157). London: Routledge.

Dahl, H. M. (2015). Regulering og velfærdsprofessionelle identitet(er). In B. Greve (Ed.), *Grundbog i socialvidenskab—5 perspektiver* (pp. 109–125). Frederiksberg: Nyt fra Samfundsvidenskaberne.

Dahl, H. M., Eurich, J., Fahnøe, K., Hawker, C., Krlev, G., Langer, A., Mildenberger, G., & Pieper, M. (2014). *Promoting innovation in social services*. Heidelberg: Heidelberg University.

Dahl, H. M., Hansen, A. E., Hansen, C. S., & Kristensen, J. E. (2015a). *Kamp og status—De lange linjer I børnehaveinstitutionens og pædagogprofessionens historie fra 1820 til 2015*. Copenhagen: U Press.

Dahl, H. M., Eskelinen, L., & Hansen, E. B. (2015b). Coexisting principles and logics of elder care: Help to self-help and consumer-oriented service. *International Journal of Social Welfare, 24*(3), 287–295.

Dahle, R. (2005). Dirty work in Norwegian health context (The case of Norway). In H. M. Dahl & T. R. Eriksen (Eds.), *Dilemmas of care in the Nordic welfare state – Continuity and change* (pp. 101–111). Aldershot: Ashgate.

Dale, H. M. (2004). Forms of governance, governmentality and the EU open method of coordination. In W. Larner & W. Walters (Eds.), *Global governmentality* (pp. 174–194). London: Routledge.

Dean, M. (1999). *Governmentality: Power and rule in modern society*. London: Sage.

Ertner, M. (2016). Hvem bestemmer hvad en gangstav skal bruges til? Et etnografisk studie af velfærdsteknologi og deres brugere. *Gerontologi, 32*(1), 8–11.

Feldman, L. (2008). Status injustice: The role of the state. In K. Olson (Ed.), *Adding insult to injury—Nancy Fraser debates her critics* (pp. 221–245). London: Verso.

Finansministeriet. (2005). *Processregularing af amter og kommuner*. Albertslund: Schultz.

Foucault, M. (1978). *The history of sexuality—An introduction*. (R. Hurley, Trans.). London: Penguin Books.

Foucault, M. (1991). Governmentality. In G. Burchell, C. Gordon, & P. Miller (Eds.), *The Foucault effect* (pp. 87–104). Chicago: The University of Chicago Press.

Foucault, M. (1996). The ethics in the concern of the self as a practice of freedom. In S. Lotringer (Ed.), *Foucault live* (pp. 433–449). New York: Semiotext(e).

Foucault, M. (1997). What is critique. In S. Lotringer & L. Hochroth (Eds.), *The politics of truth* (pp. 23–82). New York: Semiotext(e).

Fraser, N. (2008). *Scales of justice—Reimagining political space in a globalizing world*. Cambridge: Polity.

Fraser, N., & Gordon, L. (1994). A genealogy of dependency: Tracing a keyword of the U.S. welfare state. *Signs, 19*(2), 309–336.

Freidson, E. (2001). *Professionalism: The third logic*. Cambridge: Polity.

Haahr, J. H. (2004). *Governing Europe—Discourse, governmentality and European integration*. London: Routledge.

Hänsel, D. (1992). Wer ist der Professionelle? *Zeitschrift für Pädagogik, 38*(6), 873–893.

Hansen, A. M., & Kamp, A. (2016). From carers to trainers: Professional identity and body work in rehabilitative eldercare. *Gender, Work & Organization* (e-publication ahead of print). https://onlinelibrary.wiley.com/doi/10.1111/gwao.12126/epdf. Accessed 21 Dec 2016.

Hansen, M. B., & Vedung, E. (2005). *Fælles sprog i ældreplejens organisering*. Odense: Syddansk Universitetsforlag.

Hansen, E. B., Eskelinen, L., & Dahl, H. M. (2011). *Hjælp til selvhjælp eller service i hjemmeplejen—Hvordan er praksis, og er der en virkning?* Copenhagen: AKF report.

Harrington, C. (2013). Governmentality and the power of the transnational women's movement. *Studies in Social Justice, 7*(1), 47–63.

Hartman, H. (1979). The unhappy marriage of marxism and feminism. *Capital & Class, 8*, 1–33.

Hernes, H. (1987). *Welfare state and woman power—Essays in state feminism*. Oslo: Universitetsforlaget.

Højlund, H. (2004). *Markedets politiske fornuft. Et studie af velfærdens organisering i perioden 1990–2003, PhD series 17*. København: CBS.

Hoppania, H. (2015a). In a response to my question at her oral defense held on November, 2015.

Hoppania, H. (2015b). *Care as a site of political struggle, Ph.D. thesis*. Helsinki: Department of Political Science and Economic Studies.

Interview. (2013, April 24). *Focus group interview with experts conducted in Copenhagen*.

Irigaray, L. (1979). *Das Geschlecht, das nicht eins ist*. Berlin: Merve Verlag.

Irigaray, L. (1994). *Könskillnadens etik och andra texter* (C. Angelfors, Trans.). Stockholm: Brutus Östlings Bokforlag.

Johnson, T. (1995). Governmentality and the institutionalization of expertise. In T. Johnsson (Ed.), *Health professions and the state in Europe* (pp. 7–24). London: Routledge.

Kildal, N., & Nilssen, E. (2013). Ageing policy ideas in the field of health and long-term care, comparing the EU, the OECD and the WHO. In R. Ervik & T. S. Lindén (Eds.), *The making of ageing policy—Theory and practice in Europe* (pp. 53–77). Cheltenham: Edward Elgar.

Kirk, H. (1995). *Da alderen blev en diagnose.* Copenhagen: Munksgaard.

Kjær, P., & Pedersen, O. K. (2001). Translating liberalization: Neoliberalism in the Danish negotiated economy. In J. L. Campbell & O. K. Pedersen (Eds.), *The rise of neoliberalism and institutional analysis* (pp. 219–248). Princeton: Princeton University Press.

Kjellberg, R., Ibsen, R., & Kjellberg, J. (2011). *Fra pleje og omsorg til rehabilitering—viden og anbefalinger.* København: Dansk sygehus institut.

Kofod, J. (2012). hold hænderne i lommerne Om hjælp til selvhjælp på plejecentre. In M. Järvinen & N. Mik-Meyer (Ed.), *At skabe en professionel—Ansvar og autonomi i velfærdsstaten* (pp. 211–230). Copenhagen: Hans Reitzels Publishers.

Larner, W. (2000). Neo-liberalism: Policy, ideology, governmentality. *Studies in Political Economy, 63,* 5–25.

Larner, W., & Walters, W. (2004). Introduction: Global governmentality—governing international spaces. In W. Larner & W. Walters (Eds.), *Global governmentality* (pp. 1–20). London: Routledge.

Lemke, T. (2007). An indigestible meal? Foucault, governmentality and state theory. *Distinktion: Scandinavian Journal of Social Theory, 8*(2), 43–64.

Lewis, J. (Ed.). (1997). *Lone mothers in European welfare regimes.* London: Jessica Kingsley Publishers.

Lukes, S. (1974). *Power—A radical view.* Basingstoke: Macmillan.

Macleod, P., & Duurheim, K. (2002). Foucauldian feminism: The implications of governmentality. *Journal for the Theory of Social Behavior, 32*(1), 41–60.

Mahon, R. (2013). Social investment according to the OECD/DELSA: A discourse in the making. *Global Social Policy, 4*(2), 150–159.

Marcussen, M. (2002). *OECD og idespillet—Game over?* Copenhagen: Hans Reitzels publishers.

Martinsen, K. (1994). *Fra Marx til Løgstrup—om etik og sanselighed i sygeplejen.* Copenhagen: Munksgaard.

Muehlebach, A. (2012). *The moral neoliberal—Welfare and citizenship in Italy.* Chicago: University of Chicago Press.

Newman, J., & Tonkens, E. (2011). Introduction. In J. Newman & E. Tonkens (Eds.), *Participation, responsibility and choice: Summoning the active citizen in Western European welfare states* (pp. 9–28). Amsterdam: Amsterdam University Press.

Nousiainen, K. (2011). Double subsidiarity, double trouble? Allocating care responsibilities in the EU through social dialogue. In H. M. Dahl, M. Keränen, & A. Kovalainen (Eds.), *Europeanizaton, care and gender: Global complexities* (pp. 21–40). Basingstoke: Palgrave Macmillan.

Obling, A. R. (2012). Kunsten at skabe en medfølende og engageret hospitalslæge. In M. Järvinen & N. Mik-Meyer (Eds.), *At skabe en professionel—Ansvar og autonomi i velfærdsstaten* (pp. 142–164). Copenhagen: Hans Reitzels Publishers.

OECD. (2005). *Long-term care for older people?* Paris: OECD.

OECD. (2011). *Help wanted? Providing and paying for long term care.* Paris: OECD.

OECD. (2013). *A good life in old age? Monitoring and improving quality in long-term care.* Paris: OECD.

Oksala, J. (2013). Feminism and neoliberal governmentality. *Foucault Studies, 16,* 32–53.

Ong, A. (2007). Neoliberalism as a mobile technology. *Transactions of the Institute of British Geographers, 32*(1), 3–8.

Outshoorn, J., & Kantola, J. (Eds.). (2007). *Changing state feminism.* Basingstoke: Palgrave Macmillan.

Pedersen, O. K. (2011). *Konkurrencestaten.* Copenhagen: Hans Reitzels Publishers.

Poulantzas, N. (1978). *State, power and socialism.* London: Verso.

Prado, C. G. (1995). *Starting with Foucault—An introduction to genealogy.* Boulders: Westview Press.

Rasmussen, L. D. (2012). *(H)vide verden—om relationer mellem professionsidentiteter og kvalitetssikring, Ph.D. thesis.* Roskilde: Institut for samfund og globalisering.

Rönnblom, M. (2014, July 3–5). *From governance to governmentality—The need for more elaborate methodologies when studying power and politics.* Paper presented at the 9th IPA Conference, Wageningen, The Netherlands.

Sahlin-Andersson, K. (2002). National, international and transnational constructions of new public management. In T. Christensen & P. Lægreid (Eds.), *The transformation of ideas and practice* (pp. 43–72). Aldershot: Ashgate.

Sanchez, M., & Hatton-Yeo, A. (2012). Active aging and intergenerational solidarity in Europe: A conceptual reappraisal from a critical perspective. *Journal of Intergenerational Relationships, 10*(3), 276–293.

Serviceloven. (2015). *Lovbekendtgørelse number 1284 from 17/11/2015.* Social- og Indenrigsministeriet.

Søndergaard, D. M. (1994). Køn i formidlingsprocessen mellem kultur og individ: nogle analytiske greb. *Psyke & Logos, 15,* 47–68.

Soss, Fording and Schram. (2011). The organization of discipline: From performance management to perversity and punishment. *Journal of Public Administration Research and Theory, 21*(suppl. 2), 203–232.

Spanger, H. M., Dahl, H. M., & Petterson, E. (manuscript). *How do states condition care chains? Discursive framings, heterogeneous states and multilevel governance.*

Szebehely, M., & Meagher, G. (2013). Four Nordic countries—Four responses to the international trend of marketisation. In G. Meagher & M. Szebehely (Eds.), *Marketisation in Nordic eldercare* (pp. 241–288). Stockholm: Department of Social Work.

Tronto, J. (1993). *Moral boundaries: A political argument for an ethic of care.* New York: Routledge.

Thomas, T., & Davies, A. (2005). Theorizing the micro-politics of resistance: The new public management and managerial identities in the UK public service. *Organization Studies, 26*(5), 683–706.

Ulmanen, P. (2012). Working daughters: A blind spot in Swedish eldercare policy. *Social Politics, 20*(1), 65–87.

Vabö, M. (2006). Caring for people or caring for proxy consumers? *European Societies, 8*(3), 403–422.

Venogopal, R. (2015). Neoliberalism as a concept. *Economy and Society, 22*(2), 165–187.

Wærness, K. (1987). On the rationality of caring. In A. Showstack-Sassoon (Ed.), *Women and the state* (pp. 207–234). London: Hutchinson.

Walby, S. (1990). *Theorizing patriarchy.* Oxford: Basil Blackwell.

Weber, M. (1921 [1980]). *Wirtschaft und Gesellschaft.* Tübingen: Mohr Siebeck.

Witz, A. (1992). *Professions and patriarchy.* London: Routledge.

Yuval-Davis, N. (2011). *The politics of belonging – Intersectional contestations.* London: Sage.

6

Conclusion: A New Analytics

This chapter brings the insights from the previous chapters together, addressing the key question of this book: What kinds of struggles can we identify? The answer is not an exhaustive typology of different kinds of struggles in elderly care. To see and identify struggles, however, requires us to understand the changing conditions of care. Only then can we develop a new analytic of care. As the landscape of care changes, so must the theoretical discourses on care. The changing landscape requires a new analytic that can grasp the realities of care as it is politicized, regulated and becomes the subject of struggles, that is, the intensification of struggles about and within care. This new analytic—or map of elderly care—enables us to identify struggles. There are many kinds of struggles in elderly care, and various taxonomies can be used to create order and differentiation. Instead of choosing the most obvious or typical ones, I have chosen to concentrate upon two kinds of struggles that have often been neglected in care research: struggles over silencing and struggles about regulation. This chapter, going beyond the insights in the previous chapters, discusses the implications of my insights and analytic for other fields of care and other national contexts. Here I also consider new questions about elderly care from a critical perspective: In which direction

© The Author(s) 2017
H.M. Dahl, *Struggles In (Elderly) Care,*
DOI 10.1057/978-1-137-57761-0_6

is elderly care heading? What kind of challenges are we as researchers and society facing for the current form of regulation? These questions, I argue, will also be relevant for other fields and other contexts of care.

A New Analytics of Care: A Changing Landscape and a New Theorizing

As I argued in Chap. 2 care is becoming unstable and fragmented.[1] And in addition, elderly care specifically is changing. Elderly care has emerged as a national and global concern, and struggles over how to regulate elderly care have intensified. These struggles relate to the seven social and political processes that interact and frame elderly care in different ways. In this sense, there is an increasing uncertainty about who or what is responsible for caring, and an uncertainty about how to care. Care is increasingly being divided up and fragmented into bits of care, a process that reflects the professionalizing of care and its regulation under neoliberal administrative regimes. Professionalizing and neo-liberalizing pull in different directions. Whereas professionalizing care involves a division of care related to struggles about knowledge, neo-liberalizing brings marketization and privatization into the picture, changing the responsibilities and images of care—and often silencing certain kinds of care that are based upon different kinds of knowledges. Neo-liberalizing can be characterized as a process that reduces the role of knowledge in elderly care, instead stressing the practical aspects of care. Professionalizing and neo-liberalizing are processes that struggle over the role of knowledge in elderly care. But as we are also part of the processes of late modernizing, there is also an increasing reflexivity about the way in which we carry out care. Changes often bring along uncertainties about the old and the new, and in this case, cause tensions in social and political processes—and between them. One example is between commodification and late modernity. As both are ambiguous societal processes—as argued in Chap. 2—they simultaneously decrease the possibilities for emotional attachments and increase the need for emotional proximity. At the same time as these processes create uncertainty and opposing logics, care is becoming political in the broad sense of the term. The care responsibilities of society and the state are increasingly being discussed, and struggles about care proliferate.

The changing character of care, its dynamic conditions and the intensification of struggles, necessitate a rethinking of the existing analytic of care. I have suggested that we think of care in terms of relatedness instead of relations, assemblage instead of a network of care, strangers supplementing family-based care, logics replacing the analytical terms of 'dilemmas' and finally, care as part of complex emotional regimes instead of just being portrayed as 'warm hands'. Let me briefly summarize the rationales behind this alternative framework and these key terms.

Relations of care and relationships are increasingly de-stabilized and subject to change. 'Relatedness' as an analytical concept can better capture the fragility and contingency of what takes place between people across time and space. 'Relations' becomes too static a concept for our contemporary reality. The 'web of care' was earlier an adequate metaphor for the way someone in need of care was woven into relations of care, depicted as a net of closer and more distant relationships around the elderly person, without any clear beginning. The 'web of care' had a relative stability of existence. However, as relations and care relations are becoming less stable, we need to think in terms of relatedness. Care can better be described as an assemblage—an unpredictable collection of connections. In an assemblage, bodies intermingle and are part of emotional regimes (Deleuze and Guattari 1988). As part of an assemblage, care can take place or it may be absent (allowing for the potential failure of care). Instead of seeing care as provided by well-known others/family-based care, I have suggested that we include the notion of the 'stranger'. Commodifying care means that care is increasingly provided by strangers who might or might not turn into well-known others. Care workers and professional carers come and go, so care can be seen as provided by some who are known others *and* others who are strangers. Instead of seeing care as consisting of a set of relatively stable dilemmas, care is continuously enmeshed in struggles about care and about what constitutes good care. To see struggles about elderly care as 'dilemmas', embeds care in the wrong kind of frame. Struggles about elderly care cannot be framed as a question of two mutually exclusive (ethical) principles, but instead of struggles about the ideal of care. Finally, care is not just about 'warm hands' or performing care 'as if they care' (Yuval-Davis 2011: 186). Care is involved in complex assemblages and emotional regimes that prescribe and delimit proper emotions. Care assemblages govern various kinds of feelings, such as empathy, pity, disgust and uncertainty—to mention but a few. 'Emotional regimes' as a concept helps us understand the way different kinds of emotions are circulating, embedded and regulated in various contexts. In this understanding, emotions are not just existing as given reactions but engineered and regulated at various levels.

Contextualizing care in times of ongoing, often ambiguous, changes compels us to reflect upon existing theorization on elderly care. We realize that care is insufficiently theorized and cannot be grasped properly using existing theorization. Uncertainty, reflexivity and contingency lead us to rethink theorizations of care using new analytical concepts, such as relatedness, assemblage, strangers, emotional regime and logics.

Two Kinds of Struggles: Silencing and Regulation of Care

We often tend to look for struggles in a particular way. We find struggles by searching out points of tension and resistance. However, there might be struggles that we overlook. Therefore, I have suggested that we supplement the analysis of the spoken and written with an analytical attention to the silencing of elderly care—or parts of it. Silence has been taken up by philosophers such as Derrida and Foucault, and by feminist philosophers and feminist political scientists, as I argued in Chap. 4. Based upon their insights, I have argued that silence is not an entity but a process in discourse constituting—and reconstituting—the boundaries between the spoken and the silenced. Viewing silence as a process means that we must rephrase 'silence' into 'silencing' as an active verb.

Silencing can take place in two ways. Analytically, we can distinguish silencing as either dominance or subalternity. Now these are not individual features. Rather, they are characteristics of a discourse that delimits the objects, subjects and possible logics. Whereas dominance is that 'which goes without saying', for example, masculinity and whiteness, being subordinated takes place when we are unable to speak. Being without power is a characteristic of a discourse that silences those elements that have lost out in struggles. In this sense, care can be seen as something that has entered discourse, but where elements of it are silenced. In this way, discourses on care are stretched to fit existing discourses of regulation. Care becomes a parody. It is distorted by being silenced and bent to fit existing discourses. Part of this process is the *will to the pleasant,* where the unpleasant, the potentially confrontational, is silenced.

I have given examples of silencing from the Danish political-administrative discourse, such as the silencing of particular objects and particular subjects: the lonely elderly and the professional carer. But one question remains to be answered: how can we identify silencing? Traditionally, silencing has been identified using diachronic strategies such as genealogy or archeology, inspired by Foucault. These kinds of methods require historical and often large archives of material. However, I suggest alternative reading strategies that are synchronic and do not require large amounts of texts, such as comparative discourse analysis, deconstruction and memory work, discussed in Chap. 4.

Another place to look for struggles is in relation to the state and its regulation. As used here, regulation is not a synonym for implementation. Rather, it is concerned with the form of regulation and the way elderly care is regulated. There has been an intensification of regulation and in this sense an *increasing will to regulate* elderly care. Whereas some nation states have expanded their responsibility for elderly, others have restructured or retrenched their elderly care. Regardless of the kind of regulation used, European states are now paying attention to elderly care and framing it as one of their major policy issues. The framings and solutions to the 'problem of elderly care' might differ. There have been different framings of the problem, such as a care crisis, a financial burden of future generations, the lack of hands, the working conditions of paid carers or the lack of innovation in elderly care.

And there have been various solutions suggested at the global level, such as rehabilitation, increasing efficiency in elderly care, marketization or welfare technology. But despite these differences, transnational discourses on elderly care seem to have an increasing influence on the framings of problems in elderly care, both nationally and regionally. Transnational and regional discourses from WHO, OECD or the OMC in the EU help direct the attention of nation states to how they understand the problems of elderly care and also provide them with a toolbox of solutions. Despite the seductive force of transnational and regional discourses, this does not mean that it is only a one-way street from the global to the national to the local, nor does it mean that there is no resistance at various levels of regulation in reframing or changing regulatory solutions that come down from above. Regulation of elderly care has turned into a multilevel field of regulation, with players at the subnational, national and international levels. I have shown how tensions between a bureaucratic and neoliberal logic can arise, but also that various logics do not necessarily conflict. Help to self-help—a form of reablement—was translated in a way that did not conflict with the consumerist logic, and the logics were used at different times and in different settings. The multilevel, hybrid form of regulation had a potential for creating tensions that could again provide impetus to struggles about the ideal of care. Other struggles within the state take place with the introduction of neo-liberalizing. The neo-liberalizing of elderly care in the Nordic countries reveals a tightening of control through the codification of care. This relates to the passion for equality and the bureaucratic mode of regulation. Hence, the logic of neo-liberalizing co-exists with earlier logics, and in this way, the regulation of elderly care consists of a plurality of logics at different levels.

Commodifying, professionalizing and state responsibility of elderly care has changed what was previously invisible, unpaid work or precarious and unregulated care work into commodified, regulated and partly professionalized work. Regulation of elderly care, however, is still gendered. Regulation privileges 'masculinist' assumptions about elderly care, silences others and distorts care through reframing. The neoliberal discourse tends to de-professionalize care work and push it in the direction of pre-professional images of female care characterized by housework, self-sacrifice and obligingness, as I have argued in Chap. 5. The professional element in elderly care has become weaker through the neoliberal discourse—and thereby provides less recognition for caregiving work as professional work.

Beyond a Nordic Context? Beyond Elderly Care?

I have outlined the insights and the new analytic of care that are derived from a specific form of care in a specific context, that of the Nordic welfare states. Within the social sciences, there is an ongoing discussion about the delimitation of a case and the legitimacy of generalizing from case studies (Flyvbjerg 2006; Lund 2014). In the introduction, I described the material on which this book is based. I have studied the discursive regulation of elderly care in Denmark, conducted focus group interviews and observations in various municipalities in order to see first-hand the translation, resistance and lived effects of this regulation, as well as comparing my findings with research conducted by others. This is a case study of the regulation of elderly care in Denmark having studied the political-administrative discourse at the national level and chosen six focal points at the municipal level where the discourse was brought into use, translated and resisted among professional carers and elderly. This case consists of several interrelated research projects during two decades in the same country, investigating different municipalities. In this way my understanding of a case study is different from one example of a more classical understanding of a case study such as Whyte's study of street corner society and groups of young men (1993 [1943]).

In line with the Danish developmental researcher Christian Lund (2014) one could ask the question: What is this a case study of? Can we generalize the empirical and/or theoretical insights from my research on Denmark and the Nordic welfare state(s)? Can we move *beyond the Nordic context*? Empirically, Denmark and the Nordic countries are hardly typical in their welfare regime in elderly care. Denmark—like the Nordic countries generally—represents one end of a continuum in how the state has granted citizens extensive rights to receive elderly care and engineered professionalizing of care from above. Outside the Nordic countries, elderly care has been seen as something provided by either the market or by civil society (read: family and non-governmental organizations). A majority of people in Western Europe who need long-term care receive their care from relatives. Increasingly, however, unpaid work is evolving into paid care work, as the tasks of elderly care are passed on to hired domestic workers in the care chain (Lutz 2011; Isaksen 2011). This work often takes place in the domestic sphere and is therefore often 'unregulated and precarious' (Schulman et al. 2016: 3). In this way, novel architecture of elderly care created by Denmark and the other Nordic countries differs from elderly care in the rest of Europe.

However, there are social and political processes also taking place in other parts of Europe, such as commodifying, late modernizing, de-gendering and globalizing of elderly care. These processes affect elderly care along with more transnational discourses, and create change, uncertainty and ambiguity. And by doing so, they create the potential for tensions and resistance to ongoing processes. Beyond the Nordic welfare states, struggles about elderly care can also proliferate and intensify. Theoretically, my analytic, introducing concepts such as resistance, assemblage, strangers, silencing, and struggles about regulation and between different logics in elderly care has proven useful for me as a researcher. And basically, this is the litmus test of a theoretical framework: Is the theoretical map useful? Does it provide us with new understandings? This is the classical way that we judge the applicability—or area of validity—of a theoretical map in a constructivist epistemological position (Toulmin 1952; Lund 2014). Hence, we should use this analytic in different spatial and temporal contexts of elderly care and then assess whether the map is useful for studying elderly care outside the Nordic welfare states.

What about moving *beyond elderly care* to other forms of care in the Nordic welfare state? What insights can my study of Danish elderly care provide for care of preschool children or care of the sick? In my study of elderly care I have identified the proliferation of struggles, the way elements of care are silenced and some of the resistance to dominant discourses as well as the silencing of cutting sandwiches. 'Struggles', 'Resistance' and 'silencing' are conceptual tools that can help us direct our methodological and theoretical gaze so that we can assess, for example, whether struggles are also increasing in care for preschool children or for the sick within the Nordic countries. This is very likely, as these fields are also exposed to the same commodifying, professionalizing and neo-liberalizing of care as is the case in the elder sector. Preschool care, elderly care and care of the sick have become embroiled in a neo-liberalizing 'motor' that embodies a will to regulate, and toward self-responsibilizing and marketization. These processes, with all their intensity and conflicts, are bound to create tensions and struggles about forms of care in preschool and with the sick, just as they have with the elderly—also taking into account that these fields have different historical trajectories from elderly care. We have already witnessed such struggles in Denmark, with various forms of resistance among different professional groups.

Summarizing whether the theoretical map of elder care can be applied to other contexts or to non-Nordic countries is a task for other researchers to assess. Outside the Nordic context, the map is perhaps less applicable. Whereas there are similarities in relation to the social and political processes to which they are exposed, for example, globalizing, late modernizing and neo-liberalizing, there are also important differences in the role of the state between the Nordic countries and other European states.

Regulation: A New Ideal of Elderly Care and Some Reflections

European welfare regimes have developed differently in recent decades, with processes ranging from retrenchment and restructuring to an expansion of the rights of the elderly to receive care (Ranci and Pavolini 2013). Despite these differences, these various welfare regimes are all affected by a transnational discourse on elderly care and its problem(s). In this discourse, the ideal of old age is one of 'active aging'. The active aging discourse brings together ideals of healthy and successful aging (Jones and Higgs 2010). 'Active aging' as an ideal fits together with concepts such as 'reablement', 'help to self-help' or 'everyday rehabilitation', and various other ways of saying the same thing. These terms oscillate between the hope of autonomy for the elderly, a new professional identity for care workers and attempts to reduce costs for policymakers. Other key words, such as 'innovation' and 'working smarter', stem—among others—from the EU and are part of a self-referential discourse about change (reform). This discourse on change and innovation is self-referential; it does not require, indeed excludes, any further discussion or argument as to its self-evident validity. Phrased in another way: 'Innovation is good, because innovation is good'. The EU has posited itself as an 'innovation union' with a social innovation strategy and the funding of innovation projects—among others in social services—through its various research and structural funds (Dahl et al. 2014). Sometimes innovation indeed creates improvements for the elderly and reduces costs at the same time. But this is not necessarily so. And change is not always for the better. Also, the role of technology seems to be on the minds of West European policymakers (as policymakers in Eastern Europe struggle to make ends meet). Technologies are part of an imagined reduction in the number of hands, the amount of workplace injuries and costs of care. Hence, in the years to come, the key words for elderly care in Europe will be 'reablement/ rehabilitation', 'innovation' and 'technology'. We will see one 'promising solution' after another, followed by its inevitable unintended consequences.

In Denmark, the three key concepts 'reablement/rehabilitation', 'innovation' and 'technology' are already part of official policy on elderly care and have become the subject of various policy initiatives. From a critical, feminist perspective—and in the social philosophical tradition of Weber—we need to reflect upon 'the meaning of the ends we desire' (Weber 1949) and drawing on Foucault's notion of critique we need to consider questions such as: 'What are the potential problematic implications of such a policy?' I have already raised three questions of concern about the current directions of elder care policy which I will briefly summarize. One concerns the disciplining of the self in the help to self-help/ everyday rehabilitation ideology. Not all elderly wish or have the abilities to develop and keep up their abilities. A second key issue is whether re-ablement/everyday rehabilitation and help to self-help become a supplement to existing care provisions, or whether it will replace existing services, and in so doing, reveal a darker side of reablement than the more optimistic project of autonomy. Thirdly, we need to consider how this new ideal of reablement/everyday rehabilitation will change the content of care. Recent Danish research has indeed identified a new form of distanced and passive form of care. In everyday rehabilitation, this new clinical and activating focus is changing the way care is carried out (Hansen and Kamp 2016). Instead of delivering compensatory care to the elderly, there is an increasing tendency to emphasize that kind of care that aims to make the elderly more independent and self-responsible. Since not all the elderly share this urge for more independence and self-responsibility, more research is needed to investigate the effects of this new ideal of care on existing care practices.

Challenges to the Existing Forms of Regulation?

Neoliberalism and NPM have been critically assessed, both generally in the social sciences and more specifically in feminist care research concerning marketization and self-responsibilizing (Venogopal 2015; Szebehely and Meagher 2013; Dahl 2012). Neoliberalism is also a seductive force, convincing policymakers of its relevance by linking elderly care to choice, cheaper care and civil society as proving better (read: emotional) care than institutions. To regulate something requires, in turn, that it can be spoken about, delimited and fixed. However, as we have seen in the previous chapters, elderly care is contingent, complex and the object of processes of silencing. In this sense, care introduces major problems for governance, as it can be seen as constituting the limits of neoliberalism (Hoppania and Vaittinen 2015) and of regulation more generally. As I have tried to show in this book, neo-liberalizing creates problems in elderly care, and we must begin to reflect upon how to avoid these problems. We must try to do elderly care in a different way, regulated by another ideal of care.

However, the current regulation of elderly care is not exclusively a product of neoliberalism. It is produced—among others—in the interplay between neo-liberalizing and bureaucratizing processes in the Nordic welfare states, where neoliberalism has been forced to fit the institutional features of a system striving for equality and universalism. Neoliberalizing is never the only form of regulation. The current regulation of elderly care is based upon two presuppositions: that it can be regulated, and that it can be regulated in a particular way. Feminist theories of care have directly and indirectly questioned these assumptions (Hoppania and Vaittinen 2015; Mol 2008). Care and regulation have often been viewed in opposition to each other. But this needs not be the case. Elderly care has entered the social and become political; hence, it has become a domain that is necessary to regulate. This means that the problem is not regulation *per se*, but the kind of regulation that takes place.

As I discussed in Chap. 5, contemporary regulation is a hybrid form. We have seen that there are already elements of 'something' moving us beyond NPM and neo-liberalizing. This 'something' is the cross-sectoral cooperation between pillars of policy, for example, in the coordinating efforts between municipality care and the health field in the release of elderly from hospitals. These measures are intended to ease the transition from (hospitals) regional health care to municipal care to reduce the likelihood of a return to hospital and avoid care failures in the home. But not only do different logics coexist, the regulation of care is not stable. One of its logics, the neoliberal/NPM discourse is highly dynamic and co-opts new elements such as 'autonomy' and 'innovation' (Clarke and Newman 1997; Newman and Tonkens 2011). This kind of hybridity makes it methodologically difficult to distinguish between 'old' and 'new' regulation.

However, one way of thinking beyond existing ideals of care is to think along the sociological insights provided in Chap. 2. Care qualifications are changing, so we cannot rely on caring qualifications that are already existing. De-gendering reinforces this process and introduces reflexivity—and some kind of choice for women: instead of living up to social obligations, women can choose to care or perhaps not to care. One challenge, then, is to think beyond current regulation and find a way to regulate care qualifications where existing care qualifications are not neglected, but recognized, and where elderly care is (re)professionalized. Another challenge is the current tendency in a neoliberal and bureaucratized care to base regulation on distrust and adherence to standards, control, evaluation and documentation. How can we construct a regulatory regime that is less based on distrust and gives more autonomy to the care worker and the care professional? This issue is especially pertinent, in so far as self-modernizing produces self-reflective and self-realizing individuals and is thereby strongly at odds with the regime of control. Finally, current regulation is based upon the communities of care being within a nation container—or a regional container—like the EU.

However, with the increasing globalizing of elderly and care workers and professionals, this kind of cultural embedding is likely to create challenges, as the boundaries between care policies and migration are being intersected. It thus becomes difficult to regulate care, as these issues become related to who is included in the community (Sarvasy and Longo 2004): Who should we or should we not care for in a globalizing world of nomadic subjects? Instead of asking, like Hamlet: 'To be or not to be?', the existential question today becomes: *'Who should I—or we as a state—care for?'* and from the other side: *'Who will care for me?'*

I haven't dealt with these existential questions in this book. They are perhaps not altogether new, but are intensified by late modernizing and its focus upon self-realization, de-gendering, globalizing and professionalizing processes, as well as commodifying, bureaucratizing and neo-liberalizing. The two questions raised above foreground the boundaries of a given community, they concern who belongs and who does not belong. The political struggles are taking place in all parts of societies, between societies and between states. They are new kinds of meta-struggles that concern boundaries of communities and which in different frameworks have been articulated as meta-level struggles about justice (Fraser 2008) or as struggles about the politics of belonging (Yuval-Davis 2011). Meta-struggles concern the principles of who is included in the community of obligations to care. Such struggles are taking place not only in Europe and Northern America, but increasingly around the globe. The struggles about who I/we should care for concern the boundaries of the community and the responsibilities of a nation. However, with increasing regional and global migration, this issue is likely to become ever more prominent. Care is about who belongs to our community, our nation, our state. It is about who we feel related to and who we want to care for, and in what way we should care for him/her?

Note

1. As also the Austrian anthropologist Tatjana Thelen argues (2015).

References

Clarke, J., & Newman, J. (1997). *The managerial state*. London: SAGE.

Dahl, H. M. (2012). Neo-liberalism meets the Nordic welfare state—Gaps and silences. *NORA, 20*(4), 283–288.

Dahl, H. M., Eurich, J., Fahnøe, K., Hawker, C., Krlev, G., Langer, A., Mildenberger, G., & Pieper, M. (2014). *Promoting innovation in the social services—An agenda for future research and development*. Heidelberg: Baier digitaldruck.

Deleuze, G., & Guattari, F. (1988). *A thousand plateaus: Capitalism and schizophrenia*. London: The Athlone Press.

Flyvbjerg, B. (2006). Five misunderstanding of case-study research. *Qualitative Inquiry, 12*(2), 219–245.

Fraser, N. (2008). *Scales of Justice – Reimagining political space in a globalizing world*. Malden: Polity Press.

Hansen, A. M., & Kamp, A. (2016). From carers to trainers: Professional identity and body work in rehabilitative eldercare. *Gender, Work & Organization* (e-publication ahead of print). http://onlinelibrary.wiley.com/doi/10.1111/gwao.12126/epdf. Accessed 21 Dec 2016.

Hoppania, H., & Vaittinen, T. (2015). A household full of bodies: Neoliberalism, care and 'the political'. *Global Society, 29*(1), 70–88.

Isaksen, L. W. (2011). Gendering the stranger: Nomadic care workers in Europe—A Polish-Italian example. In H. M. Dahl, M. Keränen, & A. Kovalainen (Eds.), *Europeanization, care and gender: Global complexities* (pp. 141–151). Basingstoke: Palgrave Macmillan.

Jones, I. R., & Higgs, P. F. (2010). The natural, the normal and the normative: Contested terrains in ageing and old age. *Social Science and Medicine, 71*(8), 1513–1519.

Lund, C. (2014). Of what is this a case? Analytical movements in qualitative social science research. *Human Organization, 73*(3), 224–234.

Lutz, H. (2011). *The new maids: Transnational women and the care economy*. London: ZED Books.

Mol, A. (2008). *The logic of care: Health and the problem of patient choice.* London: Routledge.

Newman, J., & Tonkens, E. (2011). Introduction. In J. Newman & E. Tonkens (Eds.), *Participation, responsibility and choice: Summoning the active citizen in Western European welfare states* (pp. 9–28). Amsterdam: Amsterdam University Press.

Ranci, C., & Pavolini, E. (2013). Reforms in long-term care policies in Europe: An introduction. In C. Ranci & E. Pavolini (Eds.), *Reforms in long-term care policies in Europe: Investigating institutional change and social impacts* (pp. 3–22). Heidelberg: Springer.

Sarvasy, W., & Longo, P. (2004). The globalization of care. *International Feminist Journal of Politics, 6*(3), 392–415.

Schulman, K., Gasior, K., Fuchs, M., & Leichsenring, K. (2016). *The view from within: 'Good' care from the perspective of the care professionals—from an exploratory study, European Centre for Social Welfare Policy and Research.* Vienna: Policy Brief.

Szebehely, M., & Meagher, G. (2013). Four Nordic countries—Four responses to the international trend of marketization. In G. Meagher & M. Szebehely (Eds.), *Marketisation in Nordic elderly care: A research report on legislation, oversight, extent and consequences* (pp. 241–283). Stockholm: Department of Social Work.

Thelen, T. (2015). Care as a social organization: Creating, maintaining and dissolving significant relation. *Anthropological Theory, 15*(4), 497–515.

Toulmin, S. (1952). *The philosophy of science.* London: Hutchinson.

Venogopal, R. (2015). Neoliberalism as a concept. *Economy and Society, 22*(2), 165–187.

Weber, M. (1949). *The methodology of the social sciences.* New York: The Free Press.

Whyte, W. F. (1993 [1943]). *Street corner society.* Chicago: University of Chicago Press.

Yuval-Davis, N. (2011). *The politics of belonging: Intersectional contestations.* London: SAGE.

Index[1]

A

active ageing, 135–6, 138, 143, 145, 147, 148, 167
agency, 4–5, 10, 11, 20n3, 21n5, 29, 48, 52, 67, 71, 77, 79, 93, 95, 100, 108, 118, 121, 122, 129, 130
agents. *See* agency
archeology, 98, 108, 163
assemblage, 19, 62, 72–6, 82, 83n8, 161–2, 166

B

bureaucracy
  impartiality and rules, 29, 44
  red tape, 46–7
bureaucratizing, 3, 19, 29, 44–8, 51, 52, 121, 147, 169, 171

C

care
  care chains, 15, 20n2, 42–3, 67, 74, 166
  care crisis, 17, 27, 31, 51, 116, 163
  care qualifications, 37–8, 132, 170
  changing landscape of care, 27–54, 159–62
  codification of care, 122–3, 126, 143, 164
  compensating care, 32, 45, 53n7, 146, 169
  consumerism, 36, 122, 124, 144–6
  contextualizing care, 162
  dilemmas of care, 62, 76
  family, 2–3, 5–7, 10, 31–2, 36–8, 40, 44, 47, 73, 76–8, 81, 91, 100, 102, 119–20, 142, 146, 161, 165

[1]Note: Page numbers followed by "n" denote notes.

© The Author(s) 2017
H.M. Dahl, *Struggles In (Elderly) Care*,
DOI 10.1057/978-1-137-57761-0

care (*cont.*)
  fragmented, 73, 160
  heterotopia, 96
  hollowing out of care, 12, 50, 143
  interrelatedness, 7
  marketization, 3, 29, 30, 32, 68,
    116, 120, 134, 143, 148, 163,
    169
  relatedness, 7, 72–6, 81–2, 97,
    120, 161–2
  reproduction, 41, 105
  state responsibility of care, 2, 10,
    12, 32, 47, 76, 107, 140–2,
    164
  uncertainty, 3, 30, 32–3, 51–3,
    73, 76, 160, 162, 166
  'warm hands,' 89–90, 97, 140,
    146, 161–2
  'will to the pleasant,' 163
commodifying, 3, 19, 29–33, 51–3,
    61, 73, 161, 164, 166, 171
commodifying care, 30–3, 161
comparative, 19, 67, 98, 100–2, 108,
    109n6, 150n17, 163
critique, 46, 70–2, 75, 81, 129, 168

D

de-construction, 19, 98–100, 108,
    163
de-gendering, 3, 14, 19, 29, 38–41,
    51, 53n8, 166, 170, 171
de-professionalizing, 53n5, 142–6,
    148
dichotomies, 14, 90, 98, 109n3,
    139–42, 148, 150n19
dilemmas, 6, 7, 19, 62, 65, 76–7,
    82, 161

discourse
  analysis, 19, 92, 98, 100–2, 108,
    163
  definition, 5, 17, 91
  dynamics of discourse, 91, 124
  translation of discourse into a
    national or local context,
    16–18
  transnational discourses, 3,
    16–18, 120, 131, 135,
    149n11, 163, 166, 167
double perspective of care, 66, 68

E

emotional labor, 30–3, 53, 79
emotional regime, 14, 19, 53n4, 62,
    78–82, 83n9, 90, 144, 161–2
emotions, 8, 14, 19, 30–3, 52–3,
    53n2, 53n4, 62, 67, 69, 74–5,
    77–82, 83n9, 83n10, 90, 97,
    102, 118, 139–40, 142, 144,
    149n2, 160–2, 169
ethics of care, 62, 64–6, 76–7
European Union (EU), 2, 3, 7, 17,
    18, 39, 44, 53n6, 126, 127,
    130–2, 135–8, 148, 149n11,
    164, 168, 171
everyday rehabilitation
  characteristics, 150n14
  struggles with other logics, 134

F

family, 2, 3, 5–7, 10, 31, 32, 36–8,
    40, 44, 47, 73, 76–8, 81, 91,
    100, 102, 119, 120, 142, 146,
    161, 165

feminism, 13, 29, 39, 82n1, 90, 100, 105, 138, 140
feminist ethics of care
    Gilligan, Carol, 9–10, 64–5
    main characteristics, 7, 41
    Tronto, Joan, 15, 28, 40, 42, 63–4, 66, 96–7

G
gender
    degendering, 3, 14, 19, 29, 38–41, 51, 53n8, 166, 170–1
    femininity, 39, 41, 97, 99, 138–9, 141, 146, 148
    gendered regulation, 14, 117, 138–47, 164
    gender identity, 39–41
    gendering, 14, 38–41, 95, 139, 148, 148n1
    hegemonic masculinity, 53n9
    masculinity, 14, 39–41, 53n9, 99, 138–9, 141, 146, 163
genealogy, 98, 108, 163
globalization. See globalizing
globalizing
    families, 42–3
    time, space, 45
governance. See regulation
governmentality
    definition and characteristics, 129–30
    global governmentality, 17–18, 117, 126–38

H
home helper, 45, 69–70, 80, 102, 105–6, 118, 122–5, 134, 141, 143–7

hybrid forms of regulation, 117–26, 164, 170

L
late modern families, 36–8
late modernity. See late modernizing
late modernizing, 4, 19, 29, 36, 51, 73, 82, 160, 166–7, 171
logics
    definition, 4
    everyday rehabilitation, 146
    examples of different logics, 121
    service, 32, 49, 121, 123

M
memory work, 19, 98, 102–4, 108, 110n9, 163
multi-level governance, 117, 126–7, 132, 149n9, 149n10

N
neo-liberalism
    marketization, 73, 120, 160
    relationship bureaucracy, 76
    self-responsibilizing, 50, 73, 120, 126, 147, 169
neo-liberalizing. See neo-liberalism
New Public Management, 2, 20n1, 21n9, 32, 108, 120, 128. See also NPM
Nordic model, 9, 29
Nordic welfare state, 13, 14, 46, 51, 76, 90, 105, 106, 109n1, 120, 121, 149n12, 150n15, 165, 166, 169
NPM
    content, 48, 121

NPM (*cont.*)
  origin, 20n1

O

OECD. *See* Organization for
  Economic Co-operation and
  Development (OECD)
Open Method of Coordination
  (OMC), 18, 127, 131, 136,
  164
Organization for Economic
  Co-operation and
  Development (OECD), 3, 17,
  50, 117, 120, 130–1, 135,
  137, 138, 148, 164
outsourcing, 30–3, 47, 91

P

political, 2–5, 7–12, 15–19,
  27–30, 39–42, 46–52, 61,
  63–5, 67–8, 71, 77, 81,
  82n2, 83n6, 90–1, 96–7,
  100–2, 106, 115–16, 118,
  119, 121–3, 125, 127, 133,
  137, 140, 143, 149n9,
  149n11, 150n16, 160–3,
  165–6, 170
postmodern feminists, 95–7, 108
power
  power over, 68–70
  power to, 68–70, 93, 127, 132
professionalizing
  the professional carer, 3, 5, 11,
    15, 32–4, 41, 49–50, 53n7,
    68–9, 73–6, 78–9, 81, 97,
    104–8, 122, 133–4, 137,
    142–4, 147–8, 161, 165
  re-professionalizing, 142, 146–8

R

re-ablement. *See* everyday
  rehabilitation
recognition, 2, 33, 67, 123–6, 134,
  137, 140–2, 164
regulation
  EU, 126–7, 130–2, 135–8
  hybridity, 20, 117, 118, 138, 170
  multi-level, 18, 138, 147, 164
  OECD, 117, 120, 130–1, 135,
    137–8, 148
  Open Method of Coordination
    (OMC), 18, 127
  resistance, 7–8, 19, 68, 148,
    165–6
  and the state, 50
  WHO, 117, 135–6, 138, 148
  will to regulate, 116, 147, 163,
    167
relatedness, 7, 31, 72–6, 81, 82, 97,
  120, 161, 162
reproduction, 6, 15, 21n5, 31, 41,
  63, 105, 129
reproductive labor approach, 67
re-professionalizing, 142, 143,
  146–8

S

self-responsibilizing, 47, 49, 50, 73,
  119, 120, 126, 147, 167, 169
silence
  as an active process: silencing, 91,
    162
  comparative discourse analysis,
    19, 98, 100–2, 108, 163
  deconstruction, 19, 98–100, 108,
    163
  discursive aspects of silence, 93
  identifying silence, 91, 98, 104

memory work, 19, 98, 102–4, 108, 163
silence and speaking, 94
silence as dominance, 19, 162–3
silence as subalternity, 19, 90, 93, 162
silencing. *See* silence
social policy care literature, 67
standardizing, 5, 45, 48, 50, 51, 76, 121–3, 132–4
strangers, 19, 30, 32, 44, 53n3, 62, 72–6, 79, 82, 83n7, 161, 166
struggles
  belonging, 11
  definition, 63, 119
  within families, 7, 10
  intensification of struggles, 3–7, 68, 159, 161
  between professional groups, 7
  struggles about regulation, 19, 115–50, 159, 166
  struggles about silence, 19
  tensions and struggles, 10, 38, 77, 117, 121, 131, 134, 167

T
technology, 30, 35, 36, 42, 116, 120, 125, 130, 134, 136, 142, 149n11, 163, 168, 126, 128
transnational discourses, 3, 16–18, 120, 131, 135, 149n11, 163, 166, 167

V
valorization of care, 140, 142
vulnerability, 7, 42, 75, 96, 97, 124, 125

W
web of care, 67, 73, 161
'*What's the problem represented to be*' (WPR) approach, 98
World Health Organization (WHO), 3, 17, 117, 135, 136, 138, 148, 164

CPSIA information can be obtained
at www.ICGtesting.com
Printed in the USA
BVOW06*1735231017
498412BV00001B/10/P

9 781137 577603